Digitalised Talent Management

This book focuses on digitalised talent management—the use of information technologies in talent management. The book affords theoretically, methodologically and empirically informed insights that are especially salient given the need for executives and organisations to balance the role of humans and technology while ensuring competitiveness in this interconnected and increasingly digital world. In doing so, the book will shape and contribute to academic and industry-based conversations about the role of technological innovations in enabling organisations to transition towards digital ways of organising talent, as well as the associated implications for the who, what, where, when, and why of talent management, as stakeholders decide which aspects of talent management can be delegated to technology and those aspects which require human agency.

This book adds value by assembling subject matter experts currently siloed within traditional research domains whilst also highlighting the complexity of managing talent. By synthesising content from world-leading academics who herald from various backgrounds, the book will instigate, shape, and contribute to conversations about both the promises and perils of digitalised talent management and the extent to which judgments and decisions about an organisation's most valuable asset—it's talent—should be delegated to non-human agents.

This book will be of interest to researchers, academics and students in the fields of talent management and organisational design, especially those interested in digital ways of working, managing, and leading.

Sharna Wiblen is Assistant Professor (Lecturer) within the Sydney Business School, University of Wollongong in Sydney, Australia. Sharna blends academic skills and 15 years of industry experience including time as a management consultant, human resource and recruitment coordinator, and retail service manager to broker dialogue between academics and industry to advance the study and practice of responsible talent management.

Routledge Focus on Business and Management

Cultural Proximity and Organization
Managing Diversity and Innovation
Federica Ceci and Francesca Masciarelli

Entrepreneurial Urban Regeneration
Business Improvement Districts as a Form of Organizational Innovation
Rezart Prifti and Fatma Jaupi

Strategic University Management
Future Proofing Your Institution
Loren Falkenberg and M. Elizabeth Cannon

Innovation in Africa
Fuelling an Entrepreneurial Ecosystem for Growth and Prosperity
Deseye Umurhohwo

Consumer Behaviour and Social Network Sites
The Impact of Negative Word of Mouth
Sarah Zaraket

Artificial Intelligence in Accounting
Practical Applications
Cory Ng and John Alarcon

Digitalised Talent Management
Navigating the Human-Technology Interface
Edited by Sharna Wiblen

For more information about this series, please visit: www.routledge.com/
Routledge-Focus-on-Business-and-Management/book-series/FBM.

Digitalised Talent Management

Navigating the Human-Technology Interface

Edited by Sharna Wiblen

Routledge
Taylor & Francis Group

NEW YORK AND LONDON

First published 2021
by Routledge
52 Vanderbilt Avenue, New York, NY 10017

and by Routledge
2 Park Square, Milton Park, Abingdon, Oxon, OX14 4RN

Routledge is an imprint of the Taylor & Francis Group, an informa business

© 2021 Taylor & Francis

Library of Congress Cataloging-in-Publication Data
A catalog record for this title has been requested

ISBN: 978-0-367-21106-6 (hbk)
ISBN: 978-0-429-26544-0 (ebk)

Typeset in Times New Roman
by MPS Limited, Dehradun

To Robbie, Emmett, Sierra, and Jenson who are always on my team and forever reminding me that, while the words I write are valuable because they contribute to knowledge, it is the words I share with them every day that have the most significant impact.

Table of Contents

List of Figures

List of Tables

Acknowledgements

I acknowledge Ibraiz Tarique and extend 'many thanks' for his encouragement and contributions as I commenced on the journey of publishing this edited work.

Editor Biography

Sharna Wiblen (Ph.D.) focuses on instigating, contributing to, and shaping informed conversations that unpack the complexity of Digitalised Talent Management. Interested in how we attribute 'value' to individuals and the organisation of workforces' for strategy execution, Sharna's purpose in talking about talent is to square up the challenges associated with enacting strategically aligned talent management policies and processes and the role of digitalisation and automation in people-based activities.

Sharna's blend of skills and experiences are a rare combination: an empirical Ph.D., significant experience in attaining and executing research-based projects—with two focusing on HR technology, the ability to effectively broker dialogue with academics and executives, and 15 years of industry experience as a management consultant, human resource and recruitment coordinator, and retail service manager. Her 'talent' facilitates the advancement of knowledge while transcending the arbitrary barriers between academia and industry. Her ability to synthesise insights in the areas of talent management, HR Technology, and HR Analytics, and her empirical research on the human-technology interface is at the forefront of knowledge creation.

In addition to her role as an Associate Professor (Lecturer) within the Sydney Business School, University of Wollongong, Australia, Sharna collaborates with renowned institutions—including The Center for Effective Organizations based in Los Angeles, United States and Leeds University based in Leeds, United Kingdom. Sharna also offers presentations and executive education about talent management, workforce strategy, digitalisation, and the future of work to executives globally.

Contributors

Sophie Goodman is an Applied Anthropologist. Sophie works in organisational contexts to guide strategic decisions by bringing social science perspectives and theories to the challenges of private and public sector clients. From research-based academia to commercial management consulting, she brings a unique blend of formal qualifications and practical experience that are earned and applied across different sectors and segments. For more than a decade, Sophie has championed the value of anthropology to the world of business and to broader public life. As an applied anthropology thought leader, pioneer, and community builder, she drives impact through internal roles, client projects, and pro bono work. Sophie also serves as an industry partner and regularly Guest Lectures in Dr. Sharna Wiblen's (the Book Editor) *Responsible Talent Management Strategies* MBA subject.

Alec Levenson (Ph.D.) is a Senior Research Scientist at the University of Southern California's Center for Effective Organizations. His action research and consulting work with companies optimise organisation performance through the scientific application of organisation design, job design, human capital analytics, and strategic talent management. His work with companies combines the best elements of research and actionable knowledge that companies can use to improve performance. He draws from the disciplines of economics, strategy, organisation behaviour, and industrial-organisational psychology to tackle complex talent and organisational challenges and make recommendations on practical changes for lasting improvements.

Kristine Dery (Ph.D.) is a Research Scientist at the MIT Sloan School of Management in the Center for Information Systems Research (MIT CISR). Kristine's research in the dynamic between technology and the way people work has been a focus of her publications and teaching for the last 15 years. Kristine serves as a Senior Editor for MIS Quarterly Executive and has published in the Sloan Management Review and other leading academic and practitioner publications. Prior to her academic career, Kristine held management roles in the tourism and airline industries in Australia, New Zealand, and the United Kingdom.

Janet Marler (Ph.D.) is a Professor of Management and the Director of the HRIS Program at the School of Business at the University at Albany-State University of New York. Prior to earning a Ph.D. from Cornell University's School of Industrial and Labor Relations, she held several senior executive positions in the financial services industry. Her research on the strategic use of HR technology and HR analytics, strategic compensation, and alternative employment arrangements has been published in leading scholarly journals. With Dr. Sandra Fisher, she co-authored *Making HR Technology Decisions: A Strategic Perspective* and is also the co-editor of a future special issue on 'Digitization and the Transformation of Human Resource Management' (*International Journal of Human Resource Management*) and 'HR/People Analytics and Human Resource Management' (*Human Resource Management Journal*).

Lexy Martin is the Principal of Research and Customer Value at Visier—a people analytics solution provider. A long-time researcher, Lexy Martin is a respected thought leader and researcher on HR technology adoption and its value to organisations and workers alike. Known as the originator of the Sierra-Cedar HR Systems Survey, she now works at Visier continuing her research efforts—currently on people analytics. She works closely with customers to support them in their HR transformation to become data-driven organisations and is recognised as part of the top 100 HR Technology Influencers as selected by HR Executive Magazine.

Jeroen Meijerink (Ph.D.) is an Assistant Professor of Human Resource Management (HRM) at the University of Twente, the Netherlands. His research activities focus on HRM and value creation in the digital economy (e.g., HRM and online labour platforms/ crowdsourcing, HRM shared services, and the use of algorithms/ AI in HRM). His research has been published in peer-reviewed international outlets such as *Human Resource Management, Journal of Business Research, Human Resource Management Review, International Journal of Human Resource Management, Personnel*

Review, *European Journal of International Management,* and *The Services Industries Journal.*

Andy Charlwood (Ph.D.) is a Professor of Human Resource Management at the University of Leeds. His research interests are in HR analytics, job quality, and well-being at work. He has previously held academic posts at the Universities of Loughborough, York, and Warwick. He trained at the London School of Economics. He is a co-founder of the HR Analytics Think Tank—a network of HR practitioners and academics who want to build a robust evidence base to better understand what makes effective HR analytics. He has authored several reports on how organisations can utilise analytics for people management.

1 Digitalised Talent Management
An Introduction

Sharna Wiblen

Talent management and *digitalisation* are top priorities for organisations and senior executives (PwC, 2019, 2020). Talent management rhetoric positions *talent* as an organisation's greatest asset (Boudreau, Ramstad, & Dowling, 2002; Cushen & Thompson, 2012; Davenport, Harris, & Shapiro, 2010) worthy of proactive management and investment. At the same time, however, talent is potentially an organisation's most considerable expense (Davenport et al., 2010). Significantly, talent is essential to operational needs and strategy execution, because strategies are actualised (or not) because of the actions (or inactions) of the workforce. Organisations, regardless of size, industry, or value proposition, must 'act on their talent.'

The talk about digitalisation occurring in parallel is equally compelling. References to *digital transformation* pervade the corporate lexicon. Developments in Information Technologies (IT)—both the hardware and software—afford organisations with various options for structuring workflow processes and ways of working with 'little doubt that technology will have profound impacts on how work gets done' (Vaiman, Collings, Cascio, & Swider, 2019). Digitalisation raises many questions about human-machine work combinations and the benefits of automating tasks and occupations (Jesuthasan & Boudreau, 2018).

Talent management and technology, while salient topics in their own right, are inherently interrelated. Technology is used to manage workforces and shapes workforce structures and compositions. Newer technological innovations result in new approaches to managing talent (Wiblen, Grant, & Dery, 2010) and impact workers, jobs, and careers (Jesuthasan & Boudreau, 2018). Inversely, talent availability influences whether organisations select and deploy specific technological innovations. Neither talent nor technology, therefore, is useful in its own right. Effective talent management—the management of valuable individuals and groups of individuals—requires strategically aligned decisions and practices. Data, information, and knowledge should inform talent-based decisions and practices. Data and information are captured, stored, and analysed in conjunction with an information system—whether a pen and paper, an Excel file, a standalone or integrated human resource system (HRIS), or some other *technology.* Digital transformation, Davenport and Redman (2020) state, requires talent in four key areas: technology, data, process, and organisational change. A holistic perspective is vital because digitalisation occurs within broader systems. Appreciating both domains provides a context for reciprocity, mutual understanding, and collegiality. Thus, the talk about talent must occur with the recognition of *technology* as an actor that shapes talent management.

This book, *Digitalised Talent Management,* highlights the interrelationship between *talent management* and *technology* in an era of increasing digitalisation and automation. The book showcases how information technologies, technology-embedded and enabled frameworks, and outputs *could, should,* and *do* influence talent management. This book represents the first comprehensive discussion of the field of Digitalised Talent Management (DTM)—the use of information technology in talent management—on the market. The book frames Digitalised Talent Management in a broad sense and editorialises that it is where talent management and technology intersect. Synthesising content from various backgrounds illuminates both the promises and perils of DTM and *where* and *when* judgments and decisions about an organisation's most valuable asset—its talent—should be delegated to non-human agents, based on technologically enabled outputs or enacted via digitalised and automated processes.

Contextualising Talent Management

Talent management begins with talk about talent. Informed understandings of what talent is (or is not) are foundational to talent management strategies, policies, and practices. Organisations, via relevant stakeholders, attribute meaning to *talent* in many ways. Dominant understandings frame talent as (1) all workers and employees whereby everyone is talent, (2) specifically designated individuals, (3) specifically designated skills and capabilities, and (4) pivotal roles and positions (Wiblen, 2016; Wiblen, Dery, & Grant, 2012; Wiblen & McDonnell, 2020). Deciding *who*—which individuals and groups of individuals (talent pools)—and *what*—the defining characteristics of a talent subject (think skills, capabilities, attributes, actions)—is complex and fraught with tension. Complexity arises because talent and talent management phenomena are both socially and discursively constructed concepts with social groups deciding—and socially constructing—what talent means within the context of their social history. Organisations create and establish what talent is within the context of operational imperatives and strategic goals.

Complexity heightens as relevant stakeholders seek to reconcile inherent tensions. Tensions include whether talent is rare or everywhere; individuals are born with their talent or it can be developed; the focus should be on intelligence or competency; talent is stable or fluid; talent is about performance or potential; talent is about homogeneity (sameness) or heterogeneity (difference), and whether talent is transferable.

Further complications arise when reflecting on what talent looks like in practice. From my perspective, talent is best framed as a verb rather than a noun. Dictionaries define talent as a noun—a special aptitude; general intelligence; a person of talent or group of persons of talent in a field; or a characteristic feature, aptitude, or disposition of a person whereby an individual 'has' talent. Talent from the perspective of a verb, however, it acknowledges that we ask individuals to 'act out' their ability and illustrate their value by performing a certain way. Talented subjects (i.e., the individuals), for example, may be asked to perform above expectations and at a level higher than their peers. Talent, therefore, is a performative construct rather than a set of attributes.

Talk about *talent management* reinforces the prevailing talent tensions. Research within Strategic Human Resource Management (SHRM) and talent management is undoubtedly contested terrain as various texts focused on establishing (arbitrary) boundaries between the two research areas. Regardless of semantic and definitional differences, a more informed understanding of talent and talent management phenomena is required, as the two terms frequently feature in the corporate lexicon, with Table 1.1 offering suggestions of a few distinguishing factors.

Talent management advocates agree that *workforce differentiation* is key to talent management (see reviews of Gallardo-Gallardo & Thunnissen, 2016; McDonnell, Collings, Mellahi, & Schuler, 2017) where part of the workforce is of higher value because of their evaluated performance and/or potential. Specifically designated individuals or groups of individuals (talent pools) warrant investment through disproportionate resource allocation. Most scholars frame talent management as a set of practices focused on pivotal positions (Claussen, Grohsjean, Luger, & Probst, 2014; Collings & Mellahi, 2009; Jones, Whitaker, Seet, & Parkin, 2012; Sidani & Al Ariss, 2014). Proponents of

Table 1.1 Key Distinguishing Factors between Human Resource Management and Talent Management

Aspect	Human Resource Management	Talent Management
Who	Entire workforce	Part of the workforce
Key concepts	Procedural justice and Distributive justice	Workforce differentiation
Subjects	Everyone	Someone
Easy way to remember	Human Resource Management is about doing the same thing to everyone.	Talent Management is about doing something (a practice, resource allocation) to someone (a specific individual).

this perspective specifically advocate for the 'systematic identification' of critical positions (as per Collings & Mellahi, 2009:304) or the 'systematic attraction, identification, development, engagement/retention, and deployment of high performing and high potential employees' (as per Gallardo-Gallardo & Thunnissen, 2016:50). Talent management systems, which prioritise consistency, are most often framed as best practice and are considered the most effective (Berger & Berger, 2003; Collings & Mellahi, 2009; Iles, Chuai, & Preece, 2010; Jooss, Burbach, & Ruël, 2019). The promulgation of systematic approaches promotes procedural and distributive justice (Gelens, Hofmans, Dries, & Pepermans, 2014; Greenberg, 2002; O'Connor & Crowley-Henry, 2017) and (perceived) fairness in evaluating an individual's performance and/or potential.

Wiblen (2019:154) suggests an alternative perspective by proposing that talent management is:

> *A judgment-orientated activity where humans make judgments about the value of other humans. These judgments, while mediated by various contextual factors and variables (such as technology), should be informed by and aligned to, current and future strategic ambitions and goals.*

A judgment-based definition recognises that stakeholders use talent management—whether talent identification, talent development, or talent retention—to decide which individuals warrant additional investment. Stakeholders make judgments about the *value of individuals* within their workforces; relevant stakeholders then make *decisions* based on *judgments of value; decisions* about *resource allocations* are based on prior *judgments of value.*

Talent and talent management are contextually with each organisation required to decide *who* and *what* talent is and *how* to identify, mobilise, develop, and manage talent subjects via a set of practices within the context of their strategy. Part of this decision-making includes determining *what, where, when,* and *how* technology will feature.

Contextualising Digitalised Talent Management

Digitalised talent management—the use of information technology in talent management—permits access to pre-designed and pre-configured systems to manage workforces and talent. Since the 1990s, the terminology for HRM-focused information technologies has changed regularly as technological innovations have advanced.

Older HRIS (Human Resource Information Systems) created centralised systems that: collected, stored, and processed human resource management information (Ceriello & Freeman, 1991; Marler & Dulebohn, 2005; Stone & Dulebohn, 2013); aimed to increase HRM process and cost efficiencies (Bussler & Davis, 2001; Farndale, Paauwe, & Hoeksema, 2009; Gueutal & Stone, 2005; Ruël, Bondarouk, & Van der Velde, 2007); and promoted process consistency through automation (Benders, Batenburg, Hoeken, & Schouteten, 2006; Grant, Hall, Wailes, & Wright, 2006). Further advancements introduced internet-based self-service capabilities heralding the notion of electronic Human Resource Management (eHRM) (Marler & Fisher, 2013).

Newer technologies, as expressed through references to DTM, human capital technology, and e-talent (Wiblen, 2019), emerged alongside the rise of cloud-based technology. These innovations allow organisations to deploy specialised software at a lower cost. An added benefit is the removal of the requirement to maintain and pay for in-house IT expertise or resources (Wiblen et al., 2010) as the vendor provides such skills as part of the licensing fee (Marler & Fisher, 2017). Other compelling reasons to use technologically-enabled processes include the capacity of technology to identify talent consistently (Stahl et al., 2007); identify specific individuals worthy of developing and retaining (Lah, 2009); afford a mechanism for a talent database (Snell, 2008); improve decision-making (Lengnick-Hall & Moritz, 2003) by providing and producing information that can establish linkages between human capital assets and the performance of the business; produce dynamic, real-time metrics, analytics, and data about an organisation's human capital assets and hence talent (Williams, 2009), and facilitate faster and more accurate decision-making by harmonising human resource tasks (Parry & Tyson, 2011; Ruël, Bondarouk, & Looise, 2004; Schalk, Timmerman, & den Heuvel, 2013).

Contemporary conversations about DTM stem from the prioritisation prioritisation of systematic approaches advocated for in the talent management research noted above. Technology vendors such as SAP SuccessFactors, Oracle, Workday, etc., provide workflow processes to identify talent systematically. For a price (licensing fee), technology vendors provide performance and potential assessment criteria. Technology affords the *what* of talent management by embedding the defining characteristics of talent into the software. Technology dictates the *how* of talent management and permits the systematic and consistent evaluation where numerical scores (usually between 1 and 5 or 1 and 10) are allocated. Vendors claim that their technology facilitates faster and more accurate decision-making and gives organisations access to best practices—a set of proven or exemplary business scenarios preconfigured into the software (Yeow & Sia, 2008). For example, SAP SuccessFactors claims its software helps organisations '...to transform and expand HR strategies ... combine feedback with operational data to understand how people feel and why—and create exceptional employee experiences' (2020). Oracle's claim to fame is equally pervasive, proclaiming that its software can help organisations 'Make better decisions, personalise employee experiences...' and '...improve decisions with end-to-end talent management' (2020). With evidence of increased technology spending (PwC, 2020), we should deliberately reflect on the rhetoric, research, and the reality of DTM within the broader context of digital transformation and technology-based change.

Book Structure and Each Chapter's Contributions to the Study and Practice of Digitalised Talent Management

This book brings together a team of preeminent academics and practitioners from around the world to analyse how technologically mediated or enabled innovations are changing workplaces. The chapters provide scholars and practitioners with specific expertise in certain areas—anthropology, culture and ethnography, competency frameworks, digital talent transformations, people analytics, the gig economy, and artificial intelligence—and exposure to topics influencing how organisations *could, should,* and *do* manage workforces and talent specifically. The book also highlights the pivotal role of technology and technologically enabled processes and outputs. It incites reflection about the promise and perils associated with increased levels of digitalisation and automation whereby non-human agents are prioritised over human-based decisions and processes.

Chapter 2 Covers Anthropology, Ethnography, and Culture—Sophie Goodman

The chapter, written by **Sophie Goodman**—an **Applied Anthropologist**, previously with Deloitte—provides a foundational overview of anthropology and ethnography. Garnering a foundational perspective of anthropology is pertinent to understanding digitalised talent management. Anthropologists' signature research methodology is ethnography, which involves observing humans as they act within their natural environment. A heightened interest in ethnography arose from post-empirical research, which also included non-participant observations, highlighting how stakeholders assert that they 'know talent when they see it' (Wiblen et al., 2012). Talent performance evaluations are based on subjective interpretations of observable actions with the potential for stakeholders to derive different interpretations of the value and impact of a specific action or behaviour. I then questioned, if we 'know talent when we see it,' who teaches stakeholders how to 'see'? 'What you see, or think you see, informs your ideas and perceptions of what you think I can be.' That is, observable actions underpin talent performance, and perceptions of performance and potential inform resource allocations, promotion decisions, and career outcomes.

Gaining an informed understanding of how we see the world is of importance to both the study and practice of talent management and DTM. Many decisions about an individual's value and whether to automate processes are founded upon how individuals observe the world. We would all benefit, therefore, from investing time and resources into learning how we can see the world in a more informed way.

Furthermore, developing skills in observation and/or conducting research methodologies that include participant or non-participant observation will become essential as organisations and the stakeholders decide which decisions should be made by humans and which can be automated. Decisions about decision-making should be informed by an 'observed understanding' of how the individuals complete tasks and go about delivering on operational needs and strategy execution. Anthropology and its significant research methodology of ethnography provide a mechanism for academics and practitioners alike to generate an informed understanding of how organisational stakeholders—including individuals, teams, customers, clients, etc.—interact.

> **If I Could Say One Thing:**
> *Anthropology and its research method of ethnography help us embrace the diversity of human experience, understand perspectives different from our own, yet also reveals what binds us together as humans—all of which are vitally important as we contemplate workplaces of the future and the role of advanced technologies in them.*
> —Sophie Goodman

The chapter, by **Kristine Dery, Ph.D.**, a **Research Scientist** with the Center for Information Systems Research (CISR) within the MIT Sloan School of Management, discusses digital workplaces, digital talent, and employee experience. Unbridled access to leading companies affords Kristine and the CISR team insights about how organisations successfully transition to digital ways of working by investing in the Employee Experience (EX). Of interest is the notion that organisations should *build* rather than *buy* digital talent, thus igniting questions about how researchers and practitioners frame the value of talent acquisition in contrast to talent development.

Readers may also appreciate that digitalisation changes relationships between employees and organisations. We should not assume that the impacts of digitalisation are automatic or a given - known as technological determinism. Instead, we benefit from reflecting on the influence of digital-based change and how innovations shape and re-shape the skills and capabilities required for strategy execution (i.e. the talent). Organisations, as Kristine notes, must invest in technology and talent simultaneously to execute strategy.

Kristine's chapter contains numerous case-based examples to highlight the relationship between investing in employee experience and business outcomes. The upskilling of internal staff shows a significantly greater return than attempting to fill gaps with external talent. The value in more hybrid models, which effectively build an EX that is relevant for all employees regardless of their employment status, may provide practitioners with a clear reason why investing in internal talent and the subsequent management of internal digital talent is key to business strategy in this era of digitalisation and automation.

> **If I Could Say One Thing:**
> *Delivering the employee experience that enables digital talent to learn and grow enables firms to make effective choices to design a workforce that can deliver more value.*
> —Kristine Dery

Chapter 4 Covers the Value of Competencies—Alec Levenson

Chapter 4 considers competency models and frameworks. **Alec Levenson, Ph.D.,** a **Senior Research Scientist** with the University of Southern California's Center for Effective Organizations Name of a place, explores the value of competency frameworks. Alec Levenson's insights make numerous contributions to the study and practice of DTM. Competency frameworks underpin many talent management systems. Many organisations utilise externally designed structures for talent identification. Organisations can control the processes of evaluating performance (and potential) against the criterion—the competencies—embedded in the model. Purchasing competency models 'off the shelf' also saves costs, as responsibility for framework design resides with the vendor or provider rather than the organisation. Notably, within the context of DTM, Alec's chapter recognises the salience of competency models as a tool to control costs and processes, with standardisation promoted as a core benefit. The problem, however, is that DTM may require a focus on heterogeneity and differences rather than the sameness emphasised by competency frameworks. Although potentially strategically aligned upon implementation, the models are static and emphasise consistency. Frequently updating or iterating competency models in response to internal and external changes may be possible, but the likelihood that organisations will amend them as often as needed is improbable. Furthermore, if talent is the greatest asset, then why outsource talent competency models to an external vendor whose primary interest is to sell that framework to as many organisations as possible?

Competency frameworks focus on an individual, but most work occurs in a broader system of interrelated tasks, activities, policies, and processes. *Superior* performance, as documented in frameworks, fails to recognise that successful job, work, and task execution is a team effort. Alec does not lose this point, as he frequently reminds readers that a core limitation of competency frameworks is their frequent failure to account for team- and organisation-based factors. Today and in the future, work is a team sport. Full recognition of the team components of work, jobs, and tasks and the potential rise of the internal gig economy may initiate greater appreciation of the team-based nature of talent management.

If I Could Say One Thing:
Advancements in digital talent management have greatly increased the insights and the cost-effectiveness of using competencies, yet significant gaps remain in what can be effectively measured and managed.

—Alec Levenson

Chapter 5 Covers People Analytics and Business (Financial) Performance

Chapter 5 is about **people analytics**, a broader perspective of workforce analytics, talent analytics, data analytics, and HR analytics. **Janet H. Marler,** a **Professor** from the University at Albany-State University of New York, United States and **Lexy Martin** from **Visier, Inc.**, a technology vendor, show how advances in information technology applied to people analytics can enable organisations to document talent management's link to financial performance. Marler, a professor, and Martin, a practitioner with a technology vendor, evidence the value of academic-practitioner collaborations. Combining insights and experiences from academia and industry, Marler and Martin open their discussion of people analytics with a salient point pertinent to the study and practice of DTM—which is that vendors frequently proclaim various financial and operational benefits associated with using their products. Evidence of these positive outcomes, however, rarely accompany the pervasive assertions. Marler and Martin assert that a combination of information technology, data, and people analytics is required to validate the relationship between talent management and business (financial) performance. To prove the beneficial impacts of talent management, organisations require both information technology to capture, store, and analyse people-based data and an understanding of the role of talent in strategy execution. Furthermore, business intelligence and reporting tools associated with dashboards and scorecards are technologically enabled outputs. Simply put, people analytics is an output of DTM—the inter-relationship between information technology and talent management.

Marler and Martin offer a value chain model (Figure 5.1) after reflecting on previous cause and effect models (e.g. the LAMP Model, HR Scorecard and Balanced Scorecard, etc.) to examine the effect of HR performance drivers and enablers on financial outcomes. Establishing a beneficial relationship and a people analytics value chain involves recognising that improvements in financial performance are not immediate or technologically determined post-technology adoption. Rather, organisations adopt the technology, evolve, and iterate workplace practices to improve business outcomes. It is by improving the *doing* of talent management and then capturing the impact/outcome of intentional changes as communicated via people analytics that organisations can evaluate the impact of talent management. Testing for business-based outcomes is a process and is affected by time. That is, the value of effectively managing talent today will not be featured in people analytics and measurements until a later day. The inability to immediately capture value, however, should not detract from electing to invest in talent to realise later financial returns.

Marler and Martin's value chain model affords scholars and practitioners the guidance to start or advance on their people analytics journey. Their collaboration is an example of academic-practitioner partnerships as individuals seeking to advance the study and practice of DTM. I encourage readers to reflect on the questions posed to survey respondents and think about how they may endeavour to evaluate whether talent management is indeed beneficial for organisations.

If We Could Say One Thing:
Advancements in information technology applied to people analytics now enable organisations to more convincingly document how talent management may be linked to financial performance.
—Janet H. Marler and Lexy Martin

Chapter 6 Covers Talent Identification, Customer Reviews, and the Gig Economy—Jeroen Meijerink

Chapter 6 by **Jeroen Meijerink**, an **Assistant Professor** at the University of Twente, Netherlands, highlights the role of customers and online reviews in talent determinations within the gig economy. While there are nuances between different platforms (e.g., Uber, UberEats, MenuLog, Fiverr, etc.), the gig economy is a fruitful context to examine DTM as the organisation of work mainly occurs through technology. Jeroen's chapter usefully highlights the increasing role of customers and reviews in influencing talent status. Normative talent management discussions currently debate whether human resource professionals or line managers should be responsible for identifying, developing, and retaining talent. Explicit consideration of workforce management in the context of the gig economy, however, encourages the expansion of the *who* of talent management whereby *customers* and *algorithms* are pivotal. Customers, in leaving reviews (or not) and in allocating ratings through stars or a thumbs up/thumbs down, help determine which workers are valuable. Algorithms of each gig platform then match individuals to jobs and tasks. Algorithms also analyse reviews and ratings to rank workers. Rankings influence task/job allocation and earning ability. That is, talent management is largely enacted by customers and embedded algorithms rather than by HR and line managers. Are customers and/or algorithms considered the HR or line managers of the gig economy?

Consideration of talent identification in the gig economy reignites the inclusive versus exclusive debate. Should organisations invest in all individuals to reach their full potential or work with a select group of disproportionate benefit for strategy execution? Jeroen's chapter reflects on the value of inclusivity as platforms benefit from network effects, whereby exchanges between gig workers and customers generate fees and, therefore, revenue. Workers join with potentially minimal requirements. Minimal barriers to entry infer an inclusive approach to selecting talent. A closer examination, however, indicates that workforce differentiation and an exclusive approach occurs. Talent determinations, as noted above, result from customer reviews as platforms elect to either highlight top-rated talent or 'manage out' lower performers. Deliberate reflection on the inclusive/exclusive tension within the gig economy may provide a glimpse into the future of work as organisations elect to disaggregate traditional jobs and employees to tasks and projects.

> **If I Could Say One Thing:**
> *To understand talent identification in the gig economy, we need to understand customer reviewing behaviour and adopt a multilevel perspective on review system design, customer attributes, and gig worker performance.*
> —Jeroen Meijerink

Chapter 7 Covers the Promise and Perils of Artificial Intelligence in Various Talent Management Practices—Andy Charlwood

Chapter 7 is written by **Andy Charlwood**, a **Professor of Human Resource Management** at the University of Leeds, United Kingdom. Andy examines Artificial Intelligence (AI) as a specific form of technological innovation. The talk about AI and how this technological innovation will transform workplaces is a hot topic. While some organisations are advancing Digitalised Talent Management to include AI as part of their technology strategy, others are still grappling with how to ensure data integrity. Andy's chapter is useful, regardless of placement along the spectrum of digital transformation. Decisions about where and when to deploy the next generation of technological innovations occur within broader AI rhetoric, presenting situations where computers or robots gain delegated decision-making authority or 'take jobs away from humans.' The actualisation of such cases is fraught with complexity as an organisation navigates the challenges of implementing and enacting technology-based change—whether associated with an HRIS or AI. Andy acknowledges such complexity. In highlighting various 'barriers' and 'blockers,' we garner an informed appreciation of the dangers of deploying AI. While AI can act as a control variable, enact individual decisions automatically, and remove mundane or transactional work, AI can equally cause widespread harm. AI and the associated automation could facilitate large-scale ineffective and biased decision-making as certain ways of working and assumptions are embedded during the design phase. The dangers grow, however, as the technology automatically updates itself when new data arises. Thus, AI represents the future of talent management whereby organisations can automate effective decisions with velocity.

If I Could Say One Thing:

Ultimately, the use of AI in talent management is likely to reflect the values of the businesses introducing it and the societies they operate in. Therefore, we all have a responsibility to speak up for the values that matter to us.

—Andy Charlwood

Conclusion

Digitalised Talent Management draws on the vast expertise of the featured authors to talk about talent and to showcase the inherent interrelationship between information technology and talent management. Organisations will continually construct new ideas of which skills and capabilities are valuable, both pre- and post-technology implementations. Talking about DTM is salient because the relationship between technology and talent management is reciprocal: talent availability influences the technology organisations select and use, and technology selection and use influence the talent required to realise the benefits of digitalisation.

DTM is not a case of humans versus technology. It is, instead, about the relationship between humans and technology where they intersect in workplaces of today and the future.

If I Could Say One Thing:
Remember that we need a kaleidoscope of talent colours to make this world go 'round.
Moreover, we humans get to decide if the spectrum of technology operates in the foreground or in the background.
—Sharna Wiblen

References

Benders, J. G. J. M., Batenburg, R. S., Hoeken, P. P. W. M. & Schouteten, R. L. J. (2006). First organize, then automate: A modern socio-technical view on ERP systems and teamworking. *New Technology, Work and Employment, 21*(3), 242–251.

Berger, L. & Berger, D. (Eds.). (2003). *The talent management handbook: Creating a sustainable competitive advantage by selecting, developing and promoting the best people.* New York: McGraw-Hill Professional.

Boudreau, J. W., Ramstad, P. M. & Dowling, P. J., (2002). Global talentship: Towards a decision science connecting talent to global strategic success (CAHRS Working Paper 02–21). Retrieved from http://digitalcommons.ilr. cornell.edu/cahrswp/62/.

Bussler, L. & Davis, E., (2001). Information systems: The quiet revolution in human resource management. *Journal of Computer Information Systems, 42*(2), 17–20.

Ceriello, V. R. & Freeman, C., (1991). *Human resource management systems: Strategies, tactics and techniques.* Lexington: Lexington Books.

Claussen, J., Grohsjean, T., Luger, J. & Probst, G., (2014). Talent management and career development: What it takes to get promoted. *Journal of World Business, 49*(2), 236–244.

Collings, D. G. & Mellahi, K., (2009). Strategic talent management: A review and research agenda. *Human Resource Management Review, 19*(4), 304–313.

Cushen, J. & Thompson, P., (2012). Doing the right thing? HRM and the angry knowledge worker. *New Technology, Work and Employment, 27*(2), 79–92.

Davenport, T., Harris, J. & Shapiro, J., (2010). Competing on talent analytics. *Harvard Business Review, 88*(10), 53–58.

Davenport, T. H. & Redman, T. C., (2020). Digital transformation comes down to talent in 4 key areas. Retrieved from https://hbr.org/2020/05/digital-transformation-comes-down-to-talent-in-4-key-areas.

Farndale, E., Paauwe, J. & Hoeksema, L., (2009). In-sourcing HR: Shared service centres in the Netherlands. *International Journal of Human Resource Management, 20*(3), 544–561.

Gallardo-Gallardo, E. & Thunnissen, M., (2016). Standing on the shoulders of giants? A critical review of empirical talent management research. *Employee Relations, 38*(1), 31–56.

Gelens, J., Hofmans, J., Dries, N. & Pepermans, R., (2014). Talent management and organisational justice: Employee reactions to high potential identification. *Human Resource Management Journal, 24*(2), 159–175.

Grant, D., Hall, R., Wailes, N. & Wright, C., (2006). The false promise of technological determinism: The case of enterprise resource planning systems. *New Technology, Work & Employment, 21*(1), 2–15.

Greenberg, J., (2002). *The quest for justice on the job: Essays and experiments.* Thousand Oaks, CA: Sage Publications.

Gueutal, H. & Stone, D. L., (2005). *The brave new world of eHR: Human resources in the digital age.* San Francisco, CA: Jossey-Bass.

Iles, P., Chuai, X. & Preece, D., (2010). Talent management and HRM in multinational companies in Beijing: Definitions, differences and drivers. *Journal of World Business, 45*(2), 179–189.

Jesuthasan, R. & Boudreau, J., (2018). *Reinventing jobs: A 4-step approach for applying automation to work.* Boston, MA: Harvard Business Review Press.

Jones, J. T., Whitaker, M., Seet, P.-S. & Parkin, J., (2012). Talent management in practice in Australia: Individualistic or strategic? An exploratory study. *Asia Pacific Journal of Human Resources, 50*(4), 399–420.

Jooss, S., Burbach, R. & Ruël, H., (2019). Examining talent pools as a core talent management practice in multinational corporations. *The International Journal of Human Resource Management*, 1–32.

Lah, T. E., (2009). Using talent supply chain management to overcome challenges in the professional services market. *Workforce Management, 88*(3).

Lengnick-Hall, M. & Moritz, S., (2003). The impact of e-HR on the human resource management function. *Journal of Labor Research, 24*(3), 365–379.

Marler, J. H. & Dulebohn, J. H., (2005). *A model of employee self-service technology acceptance* (Vol. 24, pp. 137–180). Emerald Group Publishing Limited.

Marler, J. H. & Fisher, S. L., (2013). An evidence-based review of e-HRM and strategic humanresource management. *Human Resource Management Review*, *23*(1), 18–36.

Marler, J. H. & Fisher, S. L., (2017). *Making HR technology decisions: A strategic perspective.* New York: Business Expert Press, LLC.

McDonnell, A., Collings, D. G., Mellahi, K. & Schuler, R., (2017). Talent management: A systematic review and future prospects. *European Journal of International Management*, *11*(1), 86–128.

O'Connor, E. P. & Crowley-Henry, M. , (2017). Exploring the relationship between exclusive talent management, perceived organizational justice and employee engagement: Bridging the literature. *Journal of Business Ethics*, *156*(4), 903–917.

Oracle. (2020). Oracle Human Capital Management (HCM). Retrieved from https://www.oracle.com/applications/human-capital-management/.

Parry, E. & Tyson, S., (2011). Desired goals and actual outcomes of e-HRM. *Human Resource Management Journal*, *21*(3), 335–354.

PwC. (2019). Talent trends 2019: Upskilling for a digital world. *PwC's 22nd Annual Global CEO Survey.* Retrieved from https://www.pwc.com/gx/en/ceo-survey/2019/Theme-assets/reports/talent-trends-report.pdf.

PwC. (2020). 2020 HR technology survey: Key findings. Retrieved from https://www.pwc.com/us/en/library/workforce-of-the-future/hr-tech-survey.html.

Ruël, H., Bondarouk, T. & Looise, J., (2004). E-HRM: Innovation or irritation. An explorative empirical study in five large companies on web-based HRM. *Management Revue*, *15*(3), 364–380.

Ruël, H. J. M., Bondarouk, T. V. & Van der Velde, M., (2007). The contribution of e-HRM to HRM effectiveness: Results from a quantitative study in a Dutch Ministry. *Employee Relations*, *29*(3), 280–291.

Schalk, R., Timmerman, V. & den Heuvel, S. V., (2013). How strategic considerations influence decision making on e-HRM applications. *Human Resource Management Review*, *23*(1), 84–92.

Sidani, Y. & Al Ariss, A., (2014). Institutional and corporate drivers of global talent management: Evidence from the Arab Gulf region. *Journal of World Business*, *49*(2), 215–224.

Snell, A., (2008). The future of talent management. *Workforce Management*, *87*(20).

Stahl, G., Björkman, I., Farndale, E., Morris, S. S., Paauwe, J., Stiles, P., … Wright, P. M., (2007). *Global talent management: How Leading Multinationals Build and Sustain Their Talent Pipeline. INSEAD Working Papers Collection.*

Stone, D. L. & Dulebohn, J. H., (2013). Emerging issues in theory and research on electronic human resource management (eHRM). *Human Resource Management Review*, *23*(1), 1–5.

SuccessFactors, S., (2020). What is SAP SuccessFactors?. Retrieved from https://www.sap.com/australia/products/human-resources-hcm/about-successfactors.html.

Vaiman, V., Collings, D. G., Cascio, W. F. & Swider, B., (2019). *Special issue of human resource management: The shifting boundaries of talent management. Human Resource Management.*

Wiblen, S., (2016). Framing the usefulness of eHRM in talent management: A case study of talent identification in a professional services firm. *Canadian Journal of Administrative Sciences, 33*(2), 95–107.

Wiblen, S., (2019). e-Talent in talent management. In Thite, M. (Ed.). *e-HRM: Digital approaches, directions and applications* (pp. 153–171). Milton Park: Routledge.

Wiblen, S., Dery, K. & Grant, D., (2012). Do you see what I see? The role of technology in talent identification. *Asia Pacific Journal of Human Resources, 50*(4), 421–438.

Wiblen, S., Grant, D. & Dery, K., (2010). Transitioning to a new HRIS: The reshaping of human resources and information technology talent. *Journal of Electronic Commerce Research, 11*(4), 251–267.

Wiblen, S. & McDonnell, A., (2020). Connecting 'talent' meanings and multi-level context: A discursive approach. *The International Journal of Human Resource Management, 31*(4), 474–510.

Williams, H., (2009). Job analysis and HR planning. In Thite, M. & Kavanagh, M. J. (Eds.), *Human resource information systems. basics, applications, and future directions* (pp. 251–276). Thousand Oaks, CA: Sage Publications, Inc.

Yeow, A. & Sia, S. K., (2008). Negotiating 'best practices' in package software implementation. *Information and Organization, 18*(1), 1–28.

2 Anthropology, Culture, and Ethnography's Value in Understanding Digitalised Talent Management

Sophie Goodman

If I Could Say One Thing:
Anthropology and its research method of ethnography help us embrace the diversity of human experience, understand perspectives different from our own, yet also reveals what binds us together as humans, all of which are vitally important as we contemplate workplaces of the future and the role of advanced technologies in them.

—Sophie Goodman

Introduction to Anthropology

Anthropology is the academic discipline that studies the breadth of human experience. The word 'anthropology' derives from the Greek 'anthropos' word meaning human and 'logos' meaning discourse or science (Barnard, 2000). The foundational meanings of these terms highlight the ambitious remit and intent of the discipline to produce a 'science of humans.'

Anthropology is a broad, fascinating, and challenging discipline and is incredibly rewarding for those who pursue it. One of my favourite descriptions of what anthropology is and does is attributed to Ruth Benedict and has been reduced into a shareable meme-format quote: 'The purpose of anthropology is to make the world safe for human differences' (quoted in Wheeler, 2017).

For me, what sums up anthropological activity is understanding what it means to be human. Moreover, we do this by exploring similarities and differences across time and place in a neutral, informed, and prepared way. We then share those stories with others and develop theories to advance our understanding.

Anthropologists are perhaps best known for their association with culture. They have traditionally studied a range of topics related to it, including kinship, marriage, religion, power, ritual, custom, belief systems, symbols, language, myth, gender, and institutions. There are, however, four subdisciplines within anthropology:

- Archaeology which examines peoples and cultures of the past through material left behind.
- Biological anthropology specialises in evolution, genetics, forensics, and health.
- Social or cultural anthropology studies human societies and the elements of cultural life.
- Linguistic anthropology focuses on human communication and the role of language in culture.

Introduction to Culture

Founders and recognisable figures in cultural anthropology include Franz Boas, Marshal Sahlins, Margaret Mead, Ruth Benedict, Clifford Geertz, and Bronislaw Malinowski. Contemporary examples of studies into social and cultural life include Karen Ho's examination of Wall Street culture, Danny Miller's global studies on social media, and Kate Crawford's investigations into the social implications of data systems, machine learning, and artificial intelligence.

Culture Definitions

Two well-known definitions in anthropology are from Edward B. Tylor and Clifford Geertz. Both descriptions are famous (at least, in anthropology) and are an excellent starting point.

Firstly, in 1871, Tylor wrote:

> Culture, or civilisation, taken in its broad, ethnographic sense, is that complex whole which includes knowledge, belief, art, morals, law, custom, and any other capabilities and habits acquired by man as a member of society. (Tylor 1958 [1871]: 1 as cited in Monaghan & Just, 2000:35)

Contemporary culture conversations draw on this definition, particularly in management studies which often define an organisation's culture as discrete components such as beliefs, norms, and values. Clifford Geertz, almost a century later in the 1970s wrote: '…man is an animal suspended in webs of significance he himself has spun...I take culture to be those webs...' (Geertz, 1973).

This is a more typical anthropological piece of writing than Tylor's. It is beautifully descriptive but can be frustrating, because it does not give you a precise answer. If frustrated, I encourage you to reflect on it a while longer because it is insightful. For me, it points to our role in creating culture (i.e., human agency) and the stickiness of cultural phenomena (i.e., the webs) that we are surrounded and shaped by, hints to the interconnectedness of humans and the spaces they inhabit in the world, explains that context matters (otherwise you would imagine a thread and not the web), and says that we are involved in a process of sorts when we identify what has significance or meaning to us.

Across these two definitions, there are key concepts to focus on when defining culture:

- People create and comply with culture; thus, culture is a dynamic 'thing' that is continuously being formed;
- There is some agreement about the 'ingredients' of culture concerning its composition, such as beliefs, laws, customs, etc.; and
- Culture has a collective component, as in being a member of society.

Anthropological History and Evolution of the Study of 'Culture'

Anthropological topics and questions about people, their relationships with one another, and practices predate the establishment of anthropology as a distinct discipline, which most agree began around the mid-19th century (Barnard, 2000). The key theory was developed in the early 19th century by so-called 'Armchair Anthropologists' who approached the study of humans from a more philosophical standpoint before the idea of studying culture 'in the field' with those being studied (i.e., via ethnographic research) becoming prominent in the early 20th century.

To gain an idea about how anthropologists have dealt with culture so that HR generalists and practitioners can enhance their toolkit, the following section provides an overview of the concept of culture alongside key learnings that have helped to progress culture theory. Notes are included about how these ideas may apply to or are informing workplace practices, which extend beyond DTM specifically. The intention here is to deepen the reader's thinking about culture to work *in* and *on* it, rather than equip you with university-level knowledge.

Theory Overview

Evolutionism

Early attempts to study culture were influenced by Charles Darwin's theory of evolution and the publication of *On the Origin of Species* in 1859. Culture was thought to follow a similar, universal process whereby societies moved through different stages of culture from simple to complex, ultimately evolving into a 'civilised' society. Influential theorists at the time included E.B. Tylor, who proposed a three-stage, one-way direction of cultural evolution that moved from 'savagery' to 'barbarism' to 'civilisation.'

Evolutionism as an explanation of culture was heavily criticised due to the judgement of one culture over another as 'less developed' than others (often the 'advanced' culture was the one that these theorists inhabited). From such criticisms, the notion of 'ethnocentrism' formed, which is the judgement of one culture over another as somehow inferior to one's own culture. We can still see some remnants of this thinking today when we make value judgements on cultures different from our own.

Diffusionism

Culture theory has also hypothesised about both the origins of human culture and how cultural components such as customs, ideas, and practices spread or are 'diffused' from one culture to another. Many diffusionist scholars believed that humans were not innately inventive; hence, the process of cultural customs and practices diffusing and replicating outward from a handful of primary cultural hubs around the world—Egypt, for instance, was suggested—rather than being independently created. The assumption of some cultures being better or more advanced than others, unfortunately, underpinned diffusionist culture arguments. The idea that all human culture can be traced back to either a single or small group of cultures (e.g., Egypt) has largely been discredited. More contemporary, and arguably more useful, ideas have focused on how cultural practices shift and adapt as different cultures come into contact with one another.

Although anthropologists do not disagree with the idea that cultural diffusion takes place, the notion that cultural diffusion is inevitable when cultures meet each other, as diffusionists argued, is generally considered an incorrect assumption (Scupin and DeCorse, 2012 as cited in Diah, Hossain, Mustari, & Ramli, 2014). There are potentially useful learnings from diffusionist theories for HR practitioners to investigate regarding understanding how to introduce and embed new cultural traits into an organisation. Additionally, these theories could be considered when developing strategies to combine different cultures, such as those in corporate merger or acquisition scenarios, or at a smaller scale, such as when organisational business units or teams are restructured.

Structures and Functions

Functionalism, and structural-functionalism theories focus on determining if there are common or universal components that form the basis of any society and what function or role those components have in culture—particularly in meeting the needs of individual members and establishing social order. They focus on institutions such as family, education, politics, law, and religion and their role in cultural and social life. Often, an analogy of a biological organism was used to explain how the parts of a culture and their related functions contribute to or maintain the stability of the culture as a whole (Barnard, 2000) —for example, how kinship systems can promote order and solidarity.

Structuralism explored the ... idea that there are common, interconnected structures (or relationships) across all human cultures—a type of universal cultural grammar (Ortner, 1984)—meant that cultures could be 'de-coded' by comparing the composition of these common structures across different cultures.

All these theories were later criticised for an overemphasis on structure and harmony, which, it was argued, meant that their approach did not sufficiently account for the fact that cultures change. Additionally, critics argued that the focus on structure lacked consideration of actions and intentions of people within a culture—that is, human agency—and that the normal state of society was not harmony and solidarity, but, rather, contradiction and conflict (Scupin and DeCorse, 2012, as cited in Diah et al., 2014).

It is interesting to consider these criticisms concerning how culture is spoken about today, as we can often find an implicit assumption that culture's natural state is harmonious—even stable—perhaps, particularly so in large corporate cultures. Such a belief can have implications for how we think about conflict and individuals who challenge the status quo. Adopting a starting point of understanding culture as contradictory and conflicting can help to embrace the messiness that often comes with organisational life, to possibly be more open to culture change initiatives as an ongoing state rather than a moment in time, and to even reposition what a 'good' or 'healthy' culture should look like.

Culture and Personality

In the late 1920s and 1930s, theories sought to understand the relationship between personality and culture and how they inform and shape one another. Theories examined socialisation practices—namely, childrearing—across cultures to understand how the cultural environment a person is raised in can create commonalities in the personalities of its adult members.

Significant breakthroughs included Ruth Benedict, who, in 1934, proposed that cultures have certain traits or 'patterns' and that these are reflected in the personality of its members. A few years earlier, Margaret Mead concluded that cultural expectations inform an individual's development rather than biological 'truths.' For example, Mead introduced the idea that 'male' and 'female' genders were performed rather than biologically determined. Mead used her ethnographic fieldwork in other countries to show how gender can look very different in different cultures. Through her popular publications, she showed that behaviours or traits that Western nations thought of as 'masculine' or 'feminine' were not the same everywhere and were, moreover, actually determined by culture.

More broadly speaking, Benedict and Mead's groundbreaking theories helped to show how a person's cultural context influences the expression of certain character traits as 'normal' or 'appropriate.' Their works are potent reminders of the diversity rather than the universality of humans and the power of culture in forming and reinforcing behaviour.

Symbolism/Symbolic Anthropology

Symbolism emerged in the 1960s and 1970s and was a significant moment in anthropology, because it provided a shift in how culture could be studied. Culture, it was thought, was contained within symbols that represented the ideologies, beliefs, value systems, etc. of a culture. Rather than needing to get inside people's heads to understand a culture, these theorists argued that it could be understood through the study of symbols and that these symbols can be observed as people go about their lives and interact with the world.

Within this theoretical context, 'symbols' include things like language, etiquette, the built environment, costume, myth, and rituals that both reflect and shape how people see, feel, and think about the world. These symbols are ultimately vehicles for cultural meaning that communicate shared worldviews and value-orientations. Clifford

Geertz was a pioneer in developing these theories and also emphasised the importance of understanding the meaning of symbols from the viewpoint of those being studied. As Ortner states 'culture is a product of acting social beings trying to make sense of the world in which they find themselves, and if we are to make sense of a culture, we must situate ourselves in the position from which it was constructed' (1984:130).

Embodiment

Theories of culture progressed to the idea of embodiment, which raised the significance of the body as a crucial factor in cultural processes. Culture is contained and internalised in our bodies in things such as how we dress it, how we relate to it and ways we should 'appropriately' move it through space. We also need and use our bodies to understand and interact with the world around us. So, not only does culture inhabit our body and influence our actions, our bodies are actually central to how we learn and experience culture which in turn effects what and how we engage with it. One way of thinking about the vital role the body plays in learning and expressing culture is to take the idea of understanding a country or an organisation by reading a travel guide or an organisation's mission and value statements as your only input. Now think about actually going to that country or working in that organisation. The type of cultural understanding you have through the subjective bodily experience of being there and interacting with it is quite different to engaging with a culture as a 'thing' separate from you. In short, we are not just thinking beings but doing beings and theories of embodiment help us acknowledge this. Importantly, as part of this approach to culture, we need to acknowledge that our own experience of the world is also based on our own embodied culture.

The importance of observation and developing an understanding of behaviour and cultural phenomena from the viewpoint of the person/ people inhabiting a culture are core skills practiced by anthropologists today. These approaches to understanding people and their actions have extended into other professions—including user experience, design research, and employee engagement.

Formally trained and practising Anthropologists may adopt a more critical perspective of the theories covered here, as this introduction omits a more comprehensive discussion of the nuanced debates and criticisms of the evolution of anthropological theory. Instead, the intention is to afford HR practitioners with a brief understanding of the growth of the study of 'culture.'

Today, we can describe with some degree of consensus amongst cultural anthropologists that:

- Culture is a dynamic process that is both emergent (i.e., always being created) and contested (i.e., always being debated);
- Culture is a process that is deeply symbolic but is learned and shared through embodied interactions;
- There are some common structures that reinforce it—such as kinship or institutions—but those look different across cultures;
- Cultural diffusion occurs, but it is not inevitable; and
- Culture mediates behaviour.

Culture Concept in Organisations

The concept of organisational culture was introduced in the late 1970s. Management theory asserted that an organisation could have a culture and that defining an organisation's 'corporate culture' could improve operational and strategic outcomes during the 1980s (Schwartz & Davis, 1981). Definitions of what culture *is* within this context often started with Tylor's definition. Organisational culture frequently refers to the shared behaviours, values, and norms that exist within an organisation, and is often colloquially summarised as 'the way we do things around here.' It is claimed that, for management, harnessing culture can be beneficial for all manner of things that will ultimately improve the overall performance of the organisation. For this to be realised, organisations create whole departments, hire external management consultants, and/or employ change managers to define, monitor, measure, and report on culture. Almost anyone with a few years' experience in the workforce would be familiar with a transformation initiative being announced with the objective of diagnosing the culture and changing it to be what the team or wider organisation believes it needs for success.

Creating cultures and managing the process of change associated with this is big business. Numerous academic and industry-based books talk about 'culture.' There are broad global awards such as Forbes Best Company Culture, Gallup Exceptional Workplace Award, and Great Places To Work—which publicly recognise organisations with 'positive' cultures. Culture is also implicated in the success (e.g., Zappos, Southwest Airlines, Salesforce, Hilton Hotels, and Bridgewater Associates) and the 'turnaround' of organisations (e.g., Microsoft).

Culture is also framed as a negative enabler at an industry level (e.g., Australia's Royal Commission into Misconduct in the Banking, Superannuation, and Financial Services Industry), a factor in numerous high-profile corporate scandals (e.g., Volkswagen's 'Dieselgate' emissions scandal; Knowledge@Wharton, 2019), Uber's 'aggressive sales tactics' and reports of sexual harassment (Taylor & Goggin, 2017), and Wells Fargo's creation of fraudulent customer accounts to meet ambitious sales targets (Flitter, 2020), and a contributor to collapses (e.g., Enron and Lehman Brothers).

Concerning talent management specifically, job advertisements often give as much attention to describing the culture of an organisation as the role description with the culture being a key reason to apply. Thus, organisation culture can be positioned as part of an organisation's external talent management strategy and pull mechanism for attracting talent.

Key Organisational Culture Theories and Frameworks

We can see the influence of anthropological theories on the methods we use to understand organisational culture. By noting that culture can be observed, management scholars could develop frameworks to study culture systematically. Two well-known approaches are the onion and the iceberg models.

- **Onion Model:** Edgar Schein—a management professor—created the 'onion model' which includes three layers of culture, starting with basic assumptions at the centre and moving out into espoused values, artifacts, and symbols in the final layer.
- **Iceberg Model:** The 'iceberg model' is attributed to anthropologist Edward T. Hall in the 1970s. This model uses an iceberg analogy of culture, which divides iceberg aspects of culture into what can be observed (behaviours and practices) and what are unobservable (values, belief systems). It is estimated that only about 10% of the total iceberg is observable, as the majority of the iceberg exists under the surface and is unobservable. According to this model, these unobservable aspects are things like values, attitudes, and beliefs.

Both models use observable aspects such as behaviour, symbols and artifacts to understand, explain, and often change an organisation's culture. Both also acknowledge that the aspects that are harder to see—that is, at the onion's core or the iceberg under the surface of the sea—are powerful drivers of a culture and are often 'taken for granted' or are unconscious components. Hence, while these values and beliefs may be what we could say are determining or driving the observable behaviours, these can be difficult to understand with observation alone. From an anthropological perspective, this is why anthropologists typically approach research by immersing themselves in a culture to study not only the external, observable aspects of a culture, but also to learn through personal embodied experience and participation with what is under the surface and to engage with culture theory to provide a more rigorous analysis of the 'why' behind the observable behaviours, habits, and artifacts. There will be more on this approach, known as ethnography, below.

Connecting Culture to Strategy

The era of organisational culture has indeed arrived with the phrase 'culture eats strategy for breakfast' becoming well-known in HR and strategy circles. The quote is attributed to management consultant and author Peter Drucker; however, it may have been Edgar Schein who, in 1985, wrote that 'culture contains strategy,' and therefore, it is something for organisations to understand, manage and if need be, change it to better align to the stated strategy (see Quote Investigator, 2017). While it may have started with Schein, the famous mantra of culture eating strategy for breakfast gained traction in the early 2000s was attributed to Drucker in 2006 by Mark Fields. He later became chief executive of the motor company, Ford. Drucker's original writings—where he is talking about the relationship between culture and strategy—is where he purports how everything comes back to the people and the culture of the organisation which cannot be misaligned with the organisation's strategy because it will fail (Cave, 2017).

Digitalised Talent Management starts with strategy. Understanding an organisation's technology and talent management strategies includes an informed appreciation of the organisation's culture and operating procedures to work effectively with it.

From Anthropology to Ethnography

Ethnography Definitions

Ethnography is the hallmark of an anthropological approach to studying culture to understand it deeply. It is a rigorous research method underpinned by respecting the importance of context and perspective of those being investigated, making astute and systematic observations, conducting intensive and thorough analyses, and communicating those findings in a highly descriptive way to share that deep level of understanding with others (Goodman, 2018).

On a more practical note and in applied (i.e. organisational) settings, ethnography is thought of as a qualitative research method. Ethnography focuses on understanding the point of view of the person or group being studied. Individuals or groups of individuals are part of the research process with ethnographers spending time with them in their natural environment or sharing the same space, observing their actions, facilitating real-time and reflective conversations, as well as participating in daily life with them. Traditionally, ethnographic research was conducted over many years. However, in the applied context, it can be done in a few hours and supplemented with other information sources—such as personal immersion, document reviews, market scans, other secondary research sources like survey data, and so on.

While an ethnographic research project may use quantitative data, it is essentially a qualitative research method that provides the 'why' and not just the 'what' about the things people are doing, thinking, saying, believing, valuing, and creating (Goodman, 2018). Among ethnographic practitioners and academics, it can be hotly debated whether a research activity can be called ethnographic or not, and, with ethnography being discovered recently (again) by those outside of the profession, research that involves going to interview people in their home or workplace increasingly seems to be called ethnographic. However, for me, ethnographic research has specific and distinguishable qualities which include:

- The person conducting it possesses specific skills that are used to design, conduct, and make sense of the research (see qualities and skills section below);
- It occurs 'in context' of where meaning is created and what behaviours can be observed; and
- It involves observation and a degree of participation/interaction with the research topic/site and the people being studied by the researcher (Goodman, 2018).

Ethnographic Observation

An essential feature of ethnography is a type of observation called *participant observation* which combines objective, removed observer and subjective, involved participant. These approaches are two rather distinct perspectives to understanding a topic and the observations generated by them form the data gathered. The participatory aspect is where the researcher takes part in the activity or the group being studied. Participation is a matter of degree (Pelto & Pelto, 1996:68), and can range from moments and discrete interactions to sustained group membership over months or even years. While participating, the researcher observes the action, activity, or phenomenon and records that observation—including the role they played, how they felt, how they knew what to do, who they interacted with, and so on. The type of knowledge produced is different from other research methods. The experiences and feelings of the ethnographer, this *embodied* knowledge, is embraced as an essential source of data and potential insight. To truly understand the lives and perspectives of someone else, ethnographers try to *feel* these perspectives as much as possible. Ethnographic researchers will also combine this participatory and embodied information with pure observation where they adopt an almost clinical separation from the topic and people being studied, and this offers a very different viewpoint from which to learn about phenomena.

While ethnographers are skilled at pure observation, the interplay between objective observer and subjective participant through the use of participant observation is a key approach adopted by many anthropologists, because it provides information into both the above-the-surface behaviours and the below-the-surface cultural drivers to more deeply and holistically understand and make sense of those being studied. One of the most critical skills required is the ability to move between the objective observer and subjective participant to collect the different forms of data created from both approaches to produce the types of valuable insights into a culture that is famous for.

A Guide to 'Doing' Ethnography

To understand what ethnography is, it can be helpful to know the processes around how the researcher goes into 'the field,' or context to learn about a culture or people from the inside out. A useful way of thinking about the process is to describe what is done before, during, and after the research or 'fieldwork.' The following sections are an expanded version of an article written as part of the preparation for guest lectures for Dr. Wiblen's M.B.A. students.

Before: There is a whole range of activities that need to be done before fieldwork - including devising the research question, identifying the frameworks or theories that may be used, deciding how data will be recorded, gaining entry to the field site, devising safety and consent protocols, determining criteria for who to study, and arranging access to research participants, to name a few (Goodman, 2018).

During: In the field—wherever that may be, such as a group of colleagues in a workplace, customers in a bank branch, tourists in a train station, or Instagram users online—the ethnographic researcher will be observing, formally and informally speaking with people, writing and recording notes, taking photos (while always asking for permission first), and generally immersing themselves in the world of the people they want to know more about.

Due to the subjective, participatory component of ethnographic research, incorporating some degree of participation alongside the research participant is also conducted at this stage of the research process to capture what it is like for a person to, for example, complete their banking, park a car, catch public transport with a pram, or gain access to government services.

During fieldwork, ethnographers do not just casually watch people going about their business, rather, they systematically observe them. They articulate the focus of the observations and are acutely aware of the difference between an 'observation' or something that is factual and an 'inference.' If three people all saw the same thing, an observation would be the recording of that in the most factual way possible and that all three people could agree is an accurate description of what took place. An inference comes with an interpretation of what took place. Conversationally and casually, we often merge the two without realising it. Extreme forms of ill-informed observation may be considered a 'judgment.'

Ethnographers are also meticulous notetakers who capture rich, factual details in their observations during fieldwork which helps to not just limit the inferences, but also give importance to context. If you were to read an ethnographer's account of a ritual, preparation of a meal, or a shopping trip, then you would feel like you are there. We draw on all senses when describing the context in comprehensive detail. We also capture notes about the people, actions, and broader social, economic, or political systems. Note-taking is an important part of bringing others along with research conclusions, as the notes from interviews or observations are captured as neutrally and thoroughly as possible. Notes can be used as 'evidence.' It is only through the next stage in the process—conducting analysis and synthesis—that making meaning of these observations occurs.

After: As implied in the previous stage of fieldwork, ethnographic investigation produces an extensive amount of research data. This may include things like interview notes, transcripts, survey data, census information, hand-drawn pictures or photographs, video footage, and audio recordings, as well as objects and artifacts (Goodman, 2018). All this information is then thoroughly analysed. The ethnographic researcher grapples with all this data to answer the research question by coding it or breaking it down, looking for patterns, grouping commonalities, and differences, identifying points to investigate further, and analysing interesting or surprising contradictions to make sense of them.

When to Use Ethnography?

You can use ethnography when you want to understand—at a deep level—the beliefs, attitudes, behaviours, artifacts, and systems of meaning of a group of people and the contributing contextual factors. Using ethnography, you can garner insights to help:

- Record, analyse, and understand the every day, taken for granted, habitual and often unconscious activities of people;
- Explain the difference between what people say and what they do—as people can pretend and intentionally or unintentionally deceive, be unaware of their thoughts or behaviours; behave in ways that are different from what they think they do;
- Bring the employee or customer's voice into the business to help improve their experience, enhance messaging, or define future people-centred organisational strategy;
- Uncover unmet or latent needs to deliver better products or services or to create new ones; and
- Understand contextual factors that influence values, behaviour, and experience (Goodman, 2018).

Valued Skills and Qualities of an Ethnographer: The Talent Required

A range of skills and qualities are desirable for successfully undertaking and completing an ethnographic project. While qualified tertiary ethnographers have dedicated years to studying the finer points of the craft, anthropologist Brian Moeran suggests that we are all engaged in participant-observation type activities as we engage in the world and with others (2005). However, he argues that only a few actually focus on consciously applying and developing it as a practical skill (Moeran, 2005). If you want to cultivate your ethnographic skills, then I believe that the following are required to plan, conduct, and make sense of the world as an ethnographer does:

Self-Awareness

Pelto and Pelto note in their anthropological research methodology book that the ethnographer is the primary research instrument that requires 'great sensitivity and self-awareness on the part of the investigator' (1996:67). Knowing about yourself is required, so you know what biases and experiences you bring that may influence what you observe and how you interpret your fieldsite and the people within it (Goodman, 2018). You also need to be aware of how others see you, because this has an impact on how they will engage with you—for example how easily (or not) you can build rapport, how trustworthy you seem, or how knowledgeable you are about a topic, etc.

Curiosity

Genuinely being interested in the world and being open to multiple points of view means that you can research topics that you may not feel comfortable with or agree with and be effective in the field through eager exploration and inquisitive questioning. Before and after fieldwork, being curious means that you can connect research data in new ways that others have missed, reframe problems to steer effort in a more useful direction, or achieve solutions not thought of as possible with existing or default thinking (Goodman, 2018).

Critical Thinking

Ethnographers think deeply and intentionally about their research data and topic to fully make sense of it (Goodman, 2018). Ethnographers will question just about everything, including the most basic or seemingly indisputable 'truths,' interrogate assumptions, reframe a topic to find out what can be learned from another viewpoint, and apply reasoning and logic to develop their findings, insights, and recommendations for practical application to real-world problems. It is about fully evaluating all parts as well as the whole (Goodman, 2018).

Pattern Recognition

This is about noticing what is a recurring concern, point of view, experience, or behaviour across a cohort of research participants, but also extracting where there are no patterns or commonalities and whether it matters within the context of the research question that the ethnographer is tasked with (Goodman, 2018).

Intuition

This is about knowing when to follow hunches, when to back away from a question, or, alternatively, when to dig a little deeper while noticing interpersonal dynamics among research participants or between the researcher and participant and sensing what relationships or associations may hinder what is being reported (Goodman, 2018).

Empathy

Immersion into another person's worldview and experience is such a significant part of what an ethnographer must do in order to do their job well. Empathy can get mixed up with sympathy, but it is very different. For me, it is about being able to identify with another person and connect with where they are coming from, but keeping a type of neutral position. Keeping some distance prevents the ethnographer from getting too close and overidentifying with them or putting too much distance where they cannot relate (Goodman, 2018). It is not judgement. Brene Brown's short YouTube animation (Brown & Davis, 2013) is a good one if you want to look into it further. She defines empathy as *'feeling with* people' (emphasis added).

People Orientation

Since ethnographic research is about conducting research to under-stand people, being a 'people person' is pretty much a must-have. This just means that you find people interesting enough to spend a lot of time with them and to make sense of them, are able to build rapport and demonstrate trustworthiness, and put their well-being first before the project's outcomes or your project sponsor.

Communication and Storytelling

Communicating effectively with your research participants is critical, and it is essential to communicate with the stakeholders of a research project successfully. This will enable a pathway to gain access upfront to the fieldsite or win the project, as well as during the research, to share insights and disseminate findings in a compelling way (Goodman, 2018). Sharing a powerful story from the research with stakeholders can be an engaging and effective way to summarise key research findings, instil empathy for the people that have been studied, and initiate action in an organisation.

Observation

As noted earlier, ethnographers need to be both an objective observer and a subjective participant and match these two different viewpoints of the outside observer and involved participant together. That means they need keen observation skills that can note what is happening from a distance as well as while immersed within a culture.

Interviewing

Ethnographers need to be skilled interviewers who can often uncover quite subtle, intangible, and complex aspects of the human experience.

An ethnographic interview is not a typical question and answer format. It is semi-structured and more conversational in tone. It has cups of tea along the way; it moves around and changes physical location to either follow someone as they go about their day, to view an object being discussed, or to observe activity in action.

Record Management

Ethnographic research produces a lot of unstructured data, and ethnographers need to capture, store, and retrieve it to be able to rigorously analyse it and synthesise it into themes and findings with accompanying evidence.

Anthropology, Ethnography, and (Current) Digitalised Talent Management

As we build, select, and integrate new technologies into our everyday activities—including increasing digitalisation and automation in workplaces—we need to be proactive in considering contexts and behaviours which appreciate and design for 'human' experiences and endeavours. In workplaces, digitalised talent management provides organisations with enticing access to newly captured data and an advanced ability to enact decision-making with increased velocity. The realisation of the effectiveness and benefits of such technological advancements should include an informed understanding of what data is collected, how it is interpreted and by whom, what decisions are made, and what the processes are for challenging those decisions. This is particularly pertinent for talent management, as an increasing number of organisations employ software to guide, capture, store, and compute decisions about which individuals are talented and which are not.

Human resources and talent management professionals who will be interacting with digitalised talent management tools can seek to maintain the 'human' perspective in those technologies and processes by incorporating some of the approaches anthropologists use: a systems approach; embracing the breadth of human experiences, and critical thinking.

Systems thinking can help remind us about the interconnectedness of 'things'—such as material objects, environment, and people—in the world and make sense of those systems in which our organisations, workforces, and services are part of. In this respect, our organisations are both influenced by and influencing the systems they are operating within—think of things such as supply chains and trade agreements, consumer trends and behaviour patterns, natural resources, climate change, political elections and geopolitical relations, and globalisation. An awareness and appreciation of the interdependencies and relationships within a system can help to think through the impacts of organisation and workforce changes and understand the dynamics at play in living human systems. Being mindful of the decisions and actions made by key players within a system can also bolster human resource professionals' capabilities in strategic activities such as workforce planning, talent development, and recruitment.

Understanding humans and understanding the human experience in all its breadth across time and place is indispensable in order to create the experiences that we as humans seek from our work and broader social lives. While humans are frequently messy, irrational, contradictory, and even unpredictable, we need to embrace this aspect about humans to design suitable, and even optimal, organisational structures, business operating models, work environments, and roles.

At a more detailed level, part of understanding people in terms of what they say and do means placing importance on and giving due consideration to context. When language and actions are taken out of context, these can be robbed of both meaning and significance. For effective Digitalised Talent Management, this means keeping in the context of the data points collected on the activities of employees to help maintain integrity and 'truth' to data or behaviour relating to performance.

Talent management that is theoretically underpinned by an informed understanding of how humans think and act across cultures and contexts should provide us with tools, systems, and processes that serve humans, accepts variety and differences, and capitalises on our strengths. Social science and anthropology, specifically, can provide hundreds of years of theory and application help to understand humans at a deeper level—in multiple situations across cultures, time, and space.

Critical thinking is essential, as we need to garner multiple perspectives of the same phenomena and be able to strive for more objective interpretation and critique about what an observed individual or group of individuals is/are doing, what their actions and words mean, and why they talk or act in a certain way. Thinking through multiple interpretations, an awareness of various value systems, and knowledge of our preferences can help to view others with less judgement and be creative in the design and management of our organisations.

Anthropology, Ethnography, and the Future of Work

We are at a moment in our collective human history of incredible technological development. The Fourth Industrial Revolution brings some truly remarkable technologies that are both emerging and converging in compelling ways to deliver potentially rewarding human experiences and outcomes—for instance, how we could use social robots in aged care to help with social isolation and loneliness or in-home healthcare and monitoring. Artificial intelligence presents interesting opportunities in health, education, and security; virtual reality can help us design more liveable cities; autonomous drones can help safely expedite recovery efforts in natural disaster zones.

We must also pause to acknowledge the potential dark side of these types of technologies. Alongside consideration of the vast benefits is an increasing awareness of undesirable, even harmful consequences that newly emerging technologies can have. We are currently wrangling with fake news and filter bubbles spreading misinformation and disinformation, social and cultural biases being programmed into algorithms further entrenching inequality in our societies, heightened privacy concerns relating to data use and misuse and increased surveillance of citizens, and device 'addiction' and negative effects on mental health and well-being as we transition to greater levels of data collection and use and introduce new levels of automation and digitalisation. Of increasing concern is not just the individual piece of software or data set, but also the volume of decisions occurring in 'decisioning networks' as automated systems connect with one another (Evans-Greenwood, Hanson, Goodman, & Gentilin, 2020).

To responsibly embrace the potential technological opportunities, we need to pose some questions *at the very start* of automation and digitalisation processes such as: what exactly is it that we are building and why; who is it for; how might it be used for purposes different from its original intent, and who might feel the effects; what cultural or professional biases are likely to be embedded in its design, governance, and operation; what measures of success will be used; what checks should be in place, and how frequently should they occur?

Posing these questions before anything is designed or built, let alone put into action within a society, offers a stage to contemplate not only the business outcomes, but also the broader social outcomes and impacts. To do well, it requires broad input and perspectives to stimulate robust dialogue revealing organisational intentions and responsibilities. The process helps to inject a fundamentally human element into technical and commercial considerations. This is where an anthropological mindset and approaches help us critically examine and understand what it means to be human in an era of powerful technologies that inform and deliver a staggering variety of our daily experiences, including one of the places where we spend a significant amount of time in—our workplaces.

With a tendency towards increasing virtualisation of work, more and more data is becoming available on employees (Stepka, 2020). As organisations seek to make use of this data and further embed technology-enabled innovations and practices into the future workforce and workplaces, we need to be mindful that technology provides opportunities *and* obligations. Critical engagement with technological innovations—including DTM and beyond—will be fraught with complexity as we seek to learn more about our fellow humans to design technology that works best for us.

Concluding Thoughts

As we develop technology and define our workplaces of the future, there can be a tendency to compartmentalise and reduce human behaviour to neat categories and boxes. These can be helpful to get things designed and developed in organisations and put out to the marketplace, but we must remember that humans are frequently messy. They have a lot more going on in their world than behaving within a neat category of 'consumer,' 'customer,' or 'employee.' Interactions and experiences with an organisation as a customer or employee are not an isolated behaviour or action. Anthropology—the discipline that focuses on understanding the breadth and depth of human experience—offers rich understanding from both its theories and methods. Ideally the future of work will prioritise having an informed understanding of and empathy towards people, interprets behaviour within the cultural context in which it occurs and, acknowledges the significance and responsibilities of our interconnectedness to one another and the environment we inhabit. That is one which is likely to provide us with the type of rewards, technologies, and benefits that we aspire to experience in our work.

References

Barnard, A., (2000) *History and theory in anthropology*. Cambridge: Cambridge University Press.

Brown, B. & Davis, K., (2013). Brené Brown on empathy. *RSA: 21st century enlightenment.* 10 Dec 2013. Retrieved from https://www.thersa.org/discover/videos/rsa-shorts/2013/12/Brene-Brown-on-Empathy.

Cave, A., (2017). Culture eats strategy for breakfast. So what's for lunch?. *Forbes.* 9 Nov 2017. Retrieved from https://www.forbes.com/sites/andrewcave/2017/11/09/culture-eats-strategy-for-breakfast-so-whats-for-lunch/#4d1904a27e0f.

Diah, N. M., Hossain, D. M., Mustari, S. & Ramli, N. S., (2014). An overview of anthropological theories. *International Journal of Humanities and Social Science, 4*, 10(1); August 2014.

Evans-Greenwood, P., Hanson, R., Goodman, S. & Gentilin, D., A Moral License for AI: Ethics as a dialogue between firms and communities, August 2020, Deloitte Insights Deloitte Australia Centre for the Edge with the Commonwealth Scientific and Industrial Research Organisation (CSIRO).

Flitter, E., (2020). The price of Wells Fargo's fake account scandal grows by $3 billion. *The New York Times.* 21 Feb 2020. Retrieved from https://www.nytimes.com/2020/02/21/business/wells-fargo-settlement.html.

Geertz, C., (1973). *The interpretation of cultures.* New York: Basic Books.

Goodman, S., (2018). What is ethnography?. *The Applied Anthropologist.* Retrieved from https://sophiegoodmanblog.wordpress.com/2018/01/26/what-is-ethnography/.

Knowledge@Wharton. (2019). Exhausted by scandal: 'Dieselgate' continues to Haunt Volkswagen. *Knowledge@Wharton*, 21 Mar 2019. Retrieved from https://knowledge.wharton.upenn.edu/article/volkswagen-diesel-scandal/.

Moeran, B., (2005). *The business of ethnography: Strategic exchanges, people and organisations.* Berg, Oxford: Berg Publishers.

Monaghan, J. & Just, P., (2000). *Social and cultural anthropology: A very short introduction.* Oxford: Oxford University Press.

Montagnon, P., (2019). Focus on corporate culture to prevent the next scandal. strategy+business. Retrieved from https://www.strategy-business.com/article/Focus-on-corporate-culture-to-prevent-the-next-scandal?gko=63a7f.

Ortner, S. B., (1984). Theory in anthropology since the sixties. *Comparative Studies in Society and History, 26*, 126–166.

Pelto, P. J. & Pelto, G. H., (1996). *Anthropological research: The structure of inquiry* (2nd Edition). Cambridge: Cambridge University Press.

Quote Investigator. (2017). Culture eats strategy for breakfast. *Quote Investigator.* 23 May 2017. Retrieved from https://quoteinvestigator.com/2017/05/23/culture-eats/.

Schwartz, H. & Davis, S. M., (1981). Matching corporate culture and business strategy. *Organizational Dynamics, 10*, 30–48. doi:10.1016/0090-2616(81)90010-3.

Stepka, M., (2020). AI in the (increasingly virtual) workplace. *Machina Ventures.* Retrieved from https://www.machina.ventures/blog/2020/7/9/ai-in-the-increasingly-virtual-workplace.

Taylor, K. & Goggin, B., (2017). 49 of the biggest scandals in uber's history. *Business Insider, Australia.* 24 Nov 2017. Retrieved from https://www.businessinsider.com.au/uber-company-scandals-and-controversies-2017-11?r=US&IR=T.

Wheeler, R., (2017). Ruth benedict and the purpose of anthropology. *The Robert s. Peabody Institute of Archaeology.* Retrieved from https://peabody.andover.edu/2017/01/14/ruth-benedict-and-the-purpose-of-anthropology/.

3 Empowering the Workforce for Digital

Kristine Dery

If I Could Say One Thing:
Delivering the employee experience that enables digital talent to learn and grow enables firms to make effective choices to design a workforce that can deliver more value.

—Kristine Dery

Introduction

Imagine you presented your credit card to buy a new toaster, and the salesperson said your $125 purchase was declined by your bank. In the traditional world of banking, you would have to phone your bank, speak to a call center customer service agent (usually after listening 10 minutes of mind-numbing music) to try and sort out the problem.

You would want the customer service agent, with no previous knowledge of you or your credit history, to fix the problem on the spot. To add to the tension of the unknown customer and the unanticipated problem, the customer service agent is equipped with a series of scripts and a set of KPIs based on the time they take to solve the problem on the call. Technology may provide a real-time explanation for why the problem occurred (such as, automating a previously manual process that took some time), but rarely does the technology itself offer solutions. Your call is completed in a timely manner, and the agent's KPIs are met, but you are left frustrated, and your purchase is not completed.

Enter digital. Imagine the same shopping scenario, but this time, you receive a text the night before your shopping spree advising that your transactions for the day before have put your card close to capacity. A link is sent to your mobile phone enabling you to transfer funds.

With a few clicks, you solve the problem, and you are free to buy your toaster the next day without any concerns about the use of your card.

Predictive capabilities, data analytics, and mobile apps change the realm of what is possible—not only for the customer, but also for employees. Customer service people no longer waste time handling routine activities, which are increasingly dealt with using digital technologies. Humans are engaged with tasks that are less predictable and more nuanced, drawing on digital capabilities to inform and enable a better experience for the customer.

Digital technology can reimagine possibilities. As we begin to apply these new tools, we can do much more than increase the speed and efficiency of existing work. Rather, we can imagine new ways of doing things. We start to ask whether some things are best done by humans and other things by machines. However, technology itself is not the panacea. We need talent and capabilities within our organisations to make the new possibilities possible.

Companies leverage digital capabilities to design better experiences for both their employees and their customers to create value in many new ways while using different business models. Companies like DBS (a Singapore-based bank) and BBVA (an international bank based in Spain) are leveraging digital capabilities in ways that make their firms unrecognisable from the traditional and successful legacy companies that they previously were. These companies are not simply tweaking the edges; they are completely transforming the way they work to be successful in a digital world.

DBS has transformed from a company of traditional banking products to one that is 'digital to the core,' delivering employee and customer experiences via 33 digital platforms. These platforms leverage digital capabilities to deliver more predictive, value-adding banking services in ways that are easy for customers to use (Euromoney, 2019). BBVA has built and leveraged new data capabilities to design innovative products and services by applying machine learning and analytics to enable their customers to manage their lives better (2020). LTI, a Mumbai-based heavy engineering and technology firm, is investing heavily in both employee-facing technologies and skill development to enable their people to solve more complex problems for customers by combining the digital and physical worlds seamlessly (Business Wire, 2017). To realise this shift, companies like these and others have not only made significant changes to their investments in technology, but also to their abilities to build, attract, and engage the talent required to execute their strategy.

Design the Employee Experience, and They Will Come

Our study found that the large majority of companies (94%) draw on both internal and external sources of talent to varying degrees. Furthermore, an average of 60% of digital talent was employed via contracts rather than as full-time employees. The reliance on contingent talent is often based on seemingly well-founded arguments.

We hear these arguments all the time. You have heard them yourself. 'It makes more sense to use the talent from the technology vendor given their expertise.' 'Contractors give us the flexibility we need, particularly in uncertain times.' 'Current hiring restrictions mean we can get the talent we need without impacting full-time headcount.' 'We only need these specific skills to plug a gap short term.'

They are superficially attractive arguments, but an important aspect of these arguments is the supply issue. People with the digital skills that large and traditional firms need are often simply not attracted by what those firms have to offer. They prefer to work as freelancers or contractors with more freedom over where they work, which projects they work on, and how they work. Large, traditional firms often find themselves dragged unwillingly into the open labour marketplace to meet rapidly changing and growing corporate needs for digital capabilities.

Faced with a large contracted or freelance pool of talent, most of the companies in our study (53%) found it challenging to deliver an Employee Experience that integrated these people effectively into the organisation. While drawing on the external marketplace may help to plug temporary IT skills gaps and provide rapid access to talent, we found that business outcomes often suffer as a result—with higher costs, less innovation, and slower and less agile business processes.

The companies in our study did not choose to be in this position. What happened? Over time, as they joined the competitive race to deliver a better digital experience to their customers. They failed to focus the same attention on their employee experience. This meant they had two separate workforces trying to work together to solve complex digital challenges across the organisation. Each group had very different experiences of work. They had different access to training and different search capabilities. They often had different access to data, organisational systems and social networks and shared different types of knowledge. All of these factors made it hard for the two workforces to unite around shared organisational objectives.

By contrast, our research (Dery & Sebastian, 2017) showed that companies that invested in a better Employee Experience (the top 25%

of firms in our study based on their EX rating[1]) made themselves significantly more attractive to digital talent. These companies not only discovered more options around who they could employ, but they also had options around how they employed them.

We examined these high-performing EX companies based on whether they employed their digital talent as largely full-time (FTE) or largely as freelancers/contractors. FTE is a term used to describe anyone who considers themselves full-time rather than a contractor.

Companies delivering superior employee experience also performed better than their industry competitors on every measure. Not only was their net margin 10.3% higher on average, but they were also considerably faster, more agile, and more innovative than their industry competitors (Dery, van der Meulen, & Sebastian, 2018).[2]

Delivering an employee experience that is relevant for digital talent requires leaders to focus on two key aspects:

- Adaptive work environment—how well the physical and virtual workplace adapts to the needs of those working in it by leveraging technologies, data, networks, and business rules to make work easier.
- Collective work habits—how natural it is for employees to leverage the collective intelligence of the company to collaborate across silos and hierarchies, to share ideas and contribute to the new ideas of others, and to be empowered to keep redesigning better ways of getting work done.

Companies that actively focus on delivering the employee experiences that enable digital employees to thrive can be very purposeful about curating a workforce that is fit to deliver a competitive advantage in the digital world. Leaders in these companies are constantly gathering data from systems, conducting informal discussions, and using workspace sensors and many other sources to learn more about what their employees need to do their work. They are actively looking for the speedbumps that make it hard for employees to deliver value.

Understanding more about workplace speedbumps enables high-performing firms (based on their EX rating) to keep adapting their work environment to let their digital talent excel. Not only does this require a focus on how well the work environment is adapting to meet the needs of the work, but also the collective work habits that determine how naturally people are collaborating, developing new innovative ideas, and being empowered to redesign how, when, and where they work.

Digital Talent Strategies Deliver Value

To get a better understanding of how these high performing companies differ in their talent approach, we can broadly consider their talent strategies in two key categories based on whether they are largely employing their digital talent full-time or draw more from the contingent workforce. One of the factors that distinguish these strategic approaches is the way these companies approach learning and development.

High Employee Experience, Largely FTE (Enabled)

Companies following an enabled approach generate the best business outcomes on all performance measures. Enabled companies are committed to investing in their internal digital talent. Not only do these firms focus on ensuring that they support their employees with the best software and hardware to do their jobs, but they also deliver opportunities for their people to learn and grow with seamless access to data to enable evidence-based decision-making.

By building a great experience for their employees, these companies are also able to make very deliberate decisions about how they use external or contingent talent. They are more likely to make decisions about adding new skills and perspectives to enhance creativity for specified projects rather than about supplementing existing teams with the same capabilities.

Most of the companies in our study with an enabled approach to talent had intentionally designed an employee experience to shift their talent choices from being largely outsourced to largely in-sourced. To do this, these companies have built an employee experience that enables them to compete effectively for talent with digitally born companies. One of the key factors that has been instrumental in changing the options to attract more of their digital workforce full-time has been delivering a work environment where key talent can continually learn and grow.

High Employee Experience, Largely Contractors (Integrated)

Companies with an integrated approach typically describe themselves as having a workforce where it is hard to tell which talent is internally sourced and which are externally sourced. While they maintain a core of internal expertise, these companies also develop partnerships with vendors, foster relationships with talent networks, and invest in talent recruitment platforms to enhance their workforce. Integrated companies are constantly iterating to design workplaces that deliver value for their entire workforce, regardless of workers' relationship to the organisation.

While integrated companies in our research did not perform as well as those with a more enabled approach, they outperformed those firms delivering lower levels of employee experience on every measure. The difference in performance is particularly stark when we look at the 53% of companies in our study with low EX ratings and a largely external digital workforce. In these companies, not only is the net margin much lower, but they are also significantly less innovative, much slower to market, and less agile (Dery et al., 2018).

Empowering the Digital Workforce through Learning

Firms like DBS Bank in Singapore, BBVA in Spain, and a technology advisory firm called LTI in Mumbai are investing not just in deep skills of certain groups—like data analysts, coders, or UX people—but also in the broader capabilities of their entire organisation. This means that their people who have developed deep skills in digital specialties (e.g., Data Analytics) can have more meaningful conversations with broader operational teams to make better and more informed decisions. Our research strongly suggests that organisations will need to reskill their entire workforce to retain and attract the kind of talent they will need in an increasingly digital world.

BBVA

As BBVA began its journey to being a digital bank, the leadership in Madrid quickly realised that data analytics would be critical skills to advance this strategy (Wixom & Someh, 2018). These skills were not only becoming increasingly expensive to retain, but a large global bank also did not typically meet the needs of people with these skills. BBVA, like many other traditional companies, was becoming increasingly reliant on the contingent workforce for skills central to their strategy.

In 2014, BBVA introduced an internal Data Centre of Excellence designed to create a working environment to attract and retain the kind of talent with the skills critical to its digital strategy. A dedicated talent manager spent time with every employee to keep learning about what was needed to make working at a large, global bank attractive to this group of highly sought-after data analysts. Insights from this approach meant that BBVA learned how to deliver a successful strategy to enable digital talent. Not only were the digital data specialists supported with the technologies, training, and workspaces to continue to develop their talents, but BBVA was also able to invest in the data skills of all of its 130,000 employees to ensure that the specialists could effectively influence projects across the entire bank. In this way, BBVA has increasingly become attractive to the data talent it needs—providing these employees with the employee experience that enables them to deliver value and the rich learning environment that they need to grow. More recently, BBVA has been able to leverage their investment in data science talent to create the sophisticated skills they need to deliver their AI Factory and further accelerate the benefits from their data strategy (Semple, 2020).

DBS

Similarly, DBS Bank set a vision for its transformation, using the phrase 'digital to the core.' In 2009, new CEO Piyush Gupta realised that if it was to succeed in the digital world, then DBS would have to transform from a company of 22,000 traditional bankers who had been successful in the old world into a digital bank that invested heavily in different ways of delivering learning and development for its people. The transformation was so successful that DBS won the prestigious Euromoney Award for the World's Best Digital Bank in 2016 and again in 2018.

One of the most successful transformations at DBS was with middle management. Young graduates coming in at the bottom are already technology-savvy digital natives. However, above them, people who traditionally managed through command and control were now required to experiment and learn. DBS leaders had to think differently about how digital technologies could be used to transform customer experiences. The DBS strategy was to become 'digital to the core' and to do that they had to ensure that every employee had the knowledge and skills to think digitally (Dery, Sebastian, & Van der Meulen, 2016).

DBS reskilled 22,000 employees not through traditional hiring or classroom learning, but rather with experiential learning environments. It used techniques like hackathons, peer-to-peer learning, and other hands-on training to get middle management comfortable with new technologies and working in agile cross-functional teams.

The ongoing program of continuous learning across the whole bank enabled employees to have different conversations across hierarchies and business silos. As a result, DBS has moved from a largely contingent digital workforce to one where digital talent is now largely engaged through full-time employees (Sia, Weill, & Xu, 2019).

LTI

LTI—a global technology advisory company based in Mumbai—is described by its CEO as a company of 28,000 solvers. The branding 'Lets Solve IT' pervades the organisation and guides its dedicated learning program based around the Zen philosophy of Shoshin—meaning 'a beginners mindset.' Employees are encouraged to approach their learning with courage and curiosity—such qualities you might find in any beginner—and to continually build new and relevant skills to build value for both themselves and the organisation (Layak, 2019). In this way, LTI is developing deep skills and also a broader understanding to ensure that they are keeping pace with the needs of the best digital talent.

LTI has a dedicated learning and development program designed to enable every employee to challenge ideas, engage with complex problems in new ways, and leverage their new skills to actively seek new ideas and knowledge from within the organisation and through partnerships. Curiosity and learning are rewarded through a series of talent recognition programs. As employees earn new skill credentials, they are encouraged to actively deploy these skills through internal work-experience opportunities and finally move to new roles to leverage their skills. In this way, skills are targeted at all levels of the organisation to build the digital capabilities of the entire organisation. Shoshin is a key differentiator for LTI to attract and retain key digital talent as full-time employees.

Integration of Talent through Platforms

Firms that take a more hybrid approach to digital talent actively seek ways to create an employee experience that enables them to seamlessly integrate their digital talent regardless of how they are employed. Their focus is on creating an integrated learning environment to upskill their entire workforce to provide a rich environment for both full-time and contingent talent to thrive. Talent platforms are critical to these approaches enabling skill development, knowledge transfer, and cultural understanding.

Professional services companies have been experimenting with these hybrid approaches to develop better ways of engaging talent, both as FTEs and freelancers. Deloitte has built the Deloitte Open Talent Community (DOT)—a platform that provides freelancers or gig workers to engage with Deloitte projects where their skills are required. By maintaining this community on a single platform, Deloitte can provide training, on-boarding, and knowledge-sharing capabilities so that contingent talent can rapidly and effectively integrate with the full-time employees to deliver value. Talented people are provided with an environment where they can learn and grow regardless of the structure of their relationship with Deloitte.

Recommendations for Leaders

Companies that invest in an employee experience that enables their people to work more effectively will buy themselves options to curate their workforce to deliver value in a digital world. To ensure that the experience that they design and deliver is relevant to attract and retain the talent they need, they should focus on the following:

Amplify the Employee Voice

One of the best ways to build a great employee experience for digital is to amplify the voice of those employees. This needs to happen for both full-time employees and those acquired from the contingent workforce. Increased use of enterprise social media and other online platforms—physical and virtual town halls—and other ways to make it easy for diverse voices to be heard will help leaders to identify the workplace speedbumps that are making employees' lives difficult and therefore destroying value.

Gather Data from Anywhere and Everywhere

The availability of vast amounts of data is another significant trend in changing the world of work. Organisations need to gather data from wherever they can to get that data wherever it is needed. The data needs to be usable and easily understood by the people who use it.

Data can come from many sources—from conventional transactional data, from IoT sensors around workspaces, from IT help desks, and from mining unstructured data. That data should then be available to enable employees, managers, and leaders to make better decisions around building the employee experience that enables critical digital talent to thrive.

Linking the Employee Experience with Business Objectives

This means enabling people to imagine and reimagine what they need to do from an employee perspective to keep delivering value to the customer. We need to make our people fit for digital—not just so they can use different tools, but also so they can understand how existing tools can work in new ways.

Appoint an EX Leader

Dedicated leadership to identify and deliver what is required to deliver a great employee experience will ensure that resources are allocated in ways that make a difference. New metrics linking EX investments with customer value will ensure that EX is not just a nice-to-have but, rather, is a must-have sustainable set of practices central to the delivery of the digital strategy. Digital capabilities are central to the EX strategy, which means it is likely that effective leadership will be based in IT—with strong integrating skills to enable meaningful collaborations with HR, communications, and property.

Invest in Digital Skills and Sustained Learning

The ability to engage the digital talent required to advance the firm's digital transformation requires an employee experience that has a dedicated approach to upskilling the workforce for digital. High-performing firms focus on both enabling specialist digital skills to grow while, at the same time, delivering broader learning across the organisation to enable those with specialist skills to apply these effectively and thrive.

Appendix: The Research

In 2018, MIT's Center for Information Systems Research (CISR) conducted a research project designed to gain insights into how the design of the employee experience (EX) could influence the options for engaging the best digital talent. We interviewed senior executives from 28 large companies and analyzed the survey data from 279 respondents from multiple industries and geographies. While we acknowledge that digital talent is employed right across the organisation, for the purposes of this study we focused on the IT unit where the majority of digital talent are employed.

Specifically, we wanted to understand (1) the degree to which firms were sourcing their digital talent from the external marketplace rather than as full-time employees, (2) whether the employee experience offered at the impacted the mix of marketplace versus full-time digital talent, and finally, (3) whether business performance differed depending on the approach to digital talent and employee experience.

In both the qualitative and quantitative studies, we investigated the degree to which talent was sourced as contractors or gig workers versus full-time employees, the level of maturity of the employee experience in the organisation, and business performance. Additional insights were sought from the interviews to get a view into how different firms were managing digital talent, and high performing firms were explored in more detail to develop cases. Two of these cases are referred to in this chapter. Business performance was measured across four dimensions that were consistent with many of MIT CISR surveys: net margin (points above or below industry average-industry adjusted), time to market, ability to change, and innovation.

The data were analyzed according to the extent to which digital talent was full-time versus contingent and then the degree to which they had developed the EX in the organisation. The top 25% versus the rest on EX was used to identify companies that were high performing on EX versus the rest of the sample in the study. In this way, a 2 × 2 framework was identified that enabled business performance to be assessed in each quadrant.

While many researchers at MIT CISR have contributed to this research, I specifically acknowledge the research partnership and co-authorship of my colleagues—Ina Sebastian and Nick van der Meulen—who have both made a significant contribution to this data collection, analysis, and insights.

Notes

1 MIT CISR's measure of employee experience (EX) consists of two components (1) the adaptive work environment, i.e., how well the workplace adapts to the needs of the worker, and (2) the collective work habits or how natural it is for employees to leverage the collective intelligence of the company.
2 The survey data draws from the MIT CISR 2017 Pathways to Digital Business Transformation survey $N = 413$—specifically, 279 respondents provided data on their digital talent and employee experience. Net margin is industry adjusted with values as percentage points above or below the industry average, Time to market and ability to change are relative to competitors on a -100 to $+100$ scale, and innovation is the percentage of revenues from new products and services in the last three years.

References

Business Wire. (2017). L&T Infotech unveils new brand identity as LTI. *Business Wire*. 04 May 2017. Retrieved from https://www.businesswire.com/news/home/20170504005626/en/LT-Infotech-Unveils-New-Brand-Identity-LTI.

Dery, K. & Sebastian I., (2017). Building business value with employee experience. *MIT CISR Research Briefing, Number XVII-6.* 15 Jun 2017. Retrieved from https://cisr.mit.edu/publication/2017_0601_EmployeeExperience_DerySebastian.

Dery, K., Sebastian I. & Van der Meulen N., (2016). Building business value from the digital workplace. *MIT CISR Research Briefing Number XVI-9*, 15 Sep 2015. Retrieved from https://cisr.mit.edu/publication/2016_0901_DigitalWorkplaceBusinessValue_DerySebastianvanderMeulen.

Dery, K., Van der Meulen N. & Sebastian I., (2018). Employee experience: Enabling your future workforce strategy. *MIT CISR Research Briefing, Number XVIII-9*, 20 Sep 2018. Retrieved from https://cisr.mit.edu/publication/2018_0901_DigitalTalent_DeryVanderMeulenSebastian.

Euromoney. (2019). World's best bank 2019: DBS. *Euromoney.* 10 Jul 2019. Retrieved from https://www.euromoney.com/article/b1fmmkjyhws0h9/world39s-best-bank-2019-dbs.

Layak, S., (2019). How L&T Infotech is trying to leverage conglomerates strengths to leapfrog to the big league. *The Economic Times.* 06 Jan 2019. Retrieved from https://economictimes.indiatimes.com/tech/ites/how-lt-infotech-is-trying-to-leverage-conglomerates-strengths-to-leapfrog-to-the-big-league/articleshow/67400085.cms?from=mdr.

Semple, C., (2020). BBVA's data wrapping - What does it mean?. *BBVA.* 29 May 2020. Retrieved from https://www.bbva.com/en/bbvas-data-wrapping-what-does-it-mean/.

Sia, S. K., Weill P. & Xu M., (2019). DBS: From the 'World's Best Bank' to building the future ready enterprise. *MIT Center for Information Systems, Working Paper No 436.* 18 Mar 2019. Retrieved from https://cisr.mit.edu/publication/MIT_CISRwp436_DBS-FutureReadyEnterprise_SiaWeillXu.

Wixom, B. & Someh I., (2018). Accelerating data-driven transformation at BBVA. *MIT CISR Research Briefing, Number XVIII-7.* 19 Jul 2018. Retrieved from https://cisr.mit.edu/publication/2018_0701_DataDrivenBBVA_WixomSomeh.

4 Competencies in an Era of Digitalised Talent Management

Alec Levenson

If I Could Say One Thing:
Advancements in digital talent management have greatly increased the insights and the cost-effectiveness of using competencies, yet significant gaps remain in what can be effectively measured and managed.

–Alec Levenson

Introduction

McKinsey is credited with inventing the term 'talent management' in 1997 (Michaels, Handfield-Jones, & Axelrod, 2001). However, competencies have been a part of HR since the 1970s (McClelland, 1973; Spencer & Spencer, 1993). Today, competencies are a foundation of talent management in most large organisations, mainly applied to managerial work, representing the knowledge, skills, and abilities (KSAs) needed to perform the job. Today, 'talent' is what people say rather than KSAs—which explains why we seldom hear about KSAs anymore.

In recent decades, technology applications that enable digitization, automatic measurement, cataloguing and analysis of human capital and performance have advanced substantially. Today, technology provides new ways of seeing things in organisations that previously were hard to measure consistently and cost-effectively. However, for the most significant human capital and performance challenges, technology advances can create a false sense of security that all problems have been solved—triggering inaccurate talent decisions. While insights and accuracy along many dimensions have improved, substantial gaps remain.

Advances in digital talent management have not explicitly focused on competencies, but, nonetheless, provide insights about competencies' strengths and weaknesses. Advances in talent management information technology (Wiblen & Marler, 2020) have increased technology's contributions both as a control device and as a learning and feedback device. Simultaneously, risks are increasing in relying too much on technology for talent and competence decision-making.

In this chapter, I review competencies, their measurement and management via technology, and gaps in linking competencies and performance for managerial work and for work where there are extensive interdependencies. Classic challenges of talent measurement and development have grown with the rise of global supply chains and technology platforms that enable interconnections of people across time and space in ever-evolving ways.

The Origin and Application of Competencies

A full review of the history of industrial-organisational (IO) psychology leading to the modern-day competencies is beyond the scope of this chapter. A simplified accounting includes (a) using assessments for selection, (b) job analysis, and (c) the use of knowledge, skills, and abilities (KSAs) for role success.

Using assessments for selection dates back to the origins of IO psychology (Munsterberg, 1913). Assessments and job analysis have been used for a century to accurately screen and match people to roles and define role success (Dierdorff & Wilson, 2003; Ghiselli, 1973; Hunter & Hunter, 1984; Kitson, 1921; Reilly & Chao, 1982; Schmitt, Gooding, Noe, & Kirsch, 1984; Schneider & Konz 1989; Zerga, 1943).

Assessments can be developed from the job requirements, but do not have to be so. As a consequence, the United States Supreme Court in *Albemarle v. Moody* (1975) 'disallowed the use of selection tests that were designed without supporting job analysis data' (Schneider & Konz, 1989). *The Uniform Guidelines on Employee Selection Procedures* (Federal Register, 1978) cemented a foundational role for job analysis in HR (Schneider & Konz, 1989).

Assessments and job analysis are complementary—testing focuses on the person and job analysis on the role. Job analysis can identify critical tasks needed to fulfil the job requirements. Traditionally, the weakness was overly focusing on 'what' has to happen and not on 'how.' For example, operating a machine is the 'what,' and operating a machine *successfully* is the 'how.' Assessments attempt to separate those who can do the tasks from those who cannot. However, there are limits on measuring aptitude outside of working in the job even when using assessment centres and realistic job previews.

Since testing is not enough, the notion of 'knowledge, skills and abilities' (KSAs) developed over time. The origin of KSAs is partly due to some practices of the United States government. However, its ubiquity came from face validity. Each of the terms 'knowledge,' 'skills,' and 'abilities' are similar yet distinct; all three can together describe a job's full duties. Moreover, many now refer to KSAOs, where the O stands for other relevant job characteristics.

KSAs and KSAOs are a collection of different yet related things—making it hard to pin them down precisely. 'Competencies' is a single term that has roots in law, clinical psychology, vocational counselling, and education (Shippman et al., 2000)—providing the deceiving impression of being more concrete than KSAs/KSAOs. Competency models—like KSAs/KSAOs—can also be laundry lists, making them impractical to apply for evaluation or development (Campion et al., 2011). However, improved practice among scientifically-trained practitioners appears to be creating more rigorous, valid, and impactful approaches (Bartram, 2005; Campion et al., 2011; Hogan & Holland, 2003), helping to legitimize 'competencies' as a concept.

The substantive difference between KSAs and competencies is the application, especially in recent years (Campion et al., 2011). No one standard way of defining KSAs ever emerged, leaving leeway for haphazard application. Competencies, in contrast, were developed specifically to differentiate high from average performers (Spencer & Spencer, 1993)—which is more focused than the entire spectrum of potential uses for KSAs.

The difference between job requirements and competencies is the distinction between the tasks needed to be successful in a job on average, versus what distinguishes superior from average performance. Competencies are applicable to both managerial and non-managerial roles, yet the latter has not been the primary focus in recent years (Campion et al., 2011; Shippman et al., 2000). There is little controversy about the link between competencies and performance for non-managerial employees. It is usually straightforward to identify job-requirement competencies that are statistically linked to job performance.

For managerial work, in contrast, identifying competencies that can be linked to differentiated performance is much more challenging. Consequently, more attention has been paid to managerial competencies, even though, conceptually, the approach is identical (Spencer & Spencer, 1993).

Competencies as a Measure of Talent and Performing Job Duties

Recent digital advances have helped improve the measurement and management of individual, team, and organisational performance drivers, yet significant gaps persist. For both managerial and non-managerial roles, a large variation in performance remains unexplained.

The problem stems from the challenges of performance management. Kerr's (1975) timeless observation that performance management and rewards processes are riddled with measurement challenges apply equally to the questions of what talent is and what the role of competencies is. Do organisations benefit by using an imperfect measure of talent—such as competencies? Yes, if the measure improves candidate screening or promotions or guiding skills development and behaviours to improve organisational success. The downside is that everyone in the organisation may ascribe too much relevance to what can be measured, and de-emphasise other potential and more important contributors for driving organisational success.

To understand how recent advances in digital talent management are helping close the gaps, we start with the origin of competencies. Competencies arose from the need to specify job requirements rather than use standardised and intelligence tests not based on the job requirements (McClelland, 1973; Spencer & Spencer, 1993). 'Competencies' often are shorthand for the knowledge, skills, and abilities (KSAs) needed for the job. Whereas intelligence tests of general knowledge are not work-related (McClelland, Baldwin, Bronfenbrenner, & Strodtbeck, 1958), competencies are supposed to be built based on the work requirements.

For most non-managerial jobs, identifying some critical KSAs needed to perform the work is straightforward. KSAs for manual work include physical strength, stamina, and dexterity. Blue-collar work typically involves operating machinery and using tools, which can be easily documented. Office support occupations such as being an administrative assistant, in data entry, and a call center representative have well-defined KSAs. Professional jobs such as a lawyer, financial analyst, doctor, and a software coder have well-defined KSAs.

Decades of successful KSA use for non-managerial hiring and internal career paths mean that today, there is little questioning of the relevance of competencies for non-managerial jobs, in principle. However, significant limitations remain with the practice of competencies application in two areas: (a) many KSAs that are essential for non-managerial job performance cannot be easily measured, even in jobs and careers with well-established sets of KSAs, and (b) managerial work continues to elude the identification of *any* set of consistent KSAs that distinguish performance within and/or across organisations. A third challenge is that, as the world of work and organisations continues to evolve and change, today's competency models may be too backward-looking and not suited for future performance.

A lot, both positive and negative, has been written about competencies. While the development of competencies is data-based (see discussion below), the competency debate itself has been driven more by logic than voluminous evidence. It also has been practice-led, in addition to being guided by the scientific literature.

Arguments for Competencies

Advocates of competencies have some compelling arguments. First, under the broadest definition, competencies include knowledge, skills/ability, attitudes/values, and motives (Spencer & Spencer, 1993)—virtually any individual differences that may explain variation in job performance. Viewed this way, it is almost impossible to argue with the claim that competencies are better than intelligence tests for predicting job performance - one of the initial arguments for competencies (McClelland, 1973).

Competencies are usually identified by comparing successful job incumbents with others who are less successful (Spencer & Spencer, 1993). If there is a close link between technical abilities and job performance, then this approach can effectively identify successful job candidates (Hollenbeck & McCall, 2003). If any competencies can be connected to the business strategy, then including these in a competency model can be quite valuable (Spreitzer, McCall, & Mahoney, 1997).

Arguments against Competencies

The arguments against competencies are also compelling. One concern is that there are different routes to effectiveness in many jobs, so specifying a single set of competencies can be inappropriate (Drucker, 1966; Hollenbeck & McCall, 2003; McKenna, 2002). Second, most competency models are static and, thus, susceptible to changing job requirements (Hollenbeck & McCall, 2003). This is closely related to the critique that competencies typically are 'end state' characteristics, which assumes people have developed as far as they are going to (McCall, 1998). In contrast, the competencies that best predict future performance might be the ability to learn and deal with unfamiliar situations (McCall, 1998). Third, competency identification efforts often produce similar competencies across organisations, particularly for managerial jobs (Hollenbeck & McCall, 2003; Zingheim, Ledford, & Schuster, 1996), which limits their ability to be a source of competitive advantage (Lawler, 2000).

Reconciling the Arguments

The conflict between the arguments for and against competencies are most significant for more complex jobs, in particular, higher-level professional and managerial roles. Advocates argue that competency models are the most cost-effective way to select for such jobs, precisely because of their complexity (Spencer & Spencer, 1993). The critics argue that cost-effective selection does not guarantee superior performance (Hollenbeck & McCall, 2003). Both sides may be correct. Even if competencies are better than selection methods based on intelligence, task-related skills, or credentials (Spencer & Spencer, 1993), they do not tell us how, if at all, people with a given set of competencies translate that foundation into superior performance. Competency models that screen for preexisting skills may exclude candidates who will develop the skills over time while in the job and who may end up being the highest performers (McCall, 1998).

Competency advocates, in essence, rely on a statistical argument that, if certain traits are associated with better prior performance on average, then selecting based on those traits should lead to better future performance. However, the factor that distinguishes superior performance may not be having the competence but rather knowing when to apply it. For example, better communication skills should lead to better leadership. Although, this is not the same as knowing when to apply a given communication method to improve the performance of a leader's team. Taking the time to communicate critical information effectively is positive; taking too much time to communicate, in contrast, can be negative. This is the central concern with managerial or leadership competency models (Drucker, 1966; Hollenbeck & McCall, 2003).

To reconcile the arguments, consider context and the critique that most managerial competency models are the same across organisations (Hollenbeck & McCall, 1999; Zingheim, Ledford, & Schuster, 1996). Such models may be so simple that they represent the bare minimum that all managers must have for success. This, however, would run counter to the spirit of competencies, that they should differentiate superior from average performance (Spencer & Spencer, 1993). Thus, an alternative is that competencies differentiate superior from average performance in certain situations that are not universal. If so, competency models may represent a 'big tent' that encompasses the vast majority of competencies needed for successful performance across all situations, and what matters in a given situation is only a subset.

Thus there is sound logic behind the arguments both for and against competencies, as currently practiced.

Competencies and Interdependence among Roles

Another new potential critique is an over-focus on the individual rather than the team/group, organisational unit, and end-to-end organisational processes. This critique applies equally to KSAs/KSAOs, and to how most 'people-related' issues are addressed in organisations and the HR function (Levenson, 2015; Levenson, 2018). The intellectual foundation goes back decades and includes organisational diagnosis and systems thinking (Burke & Litwin, 1992; Falletta & Combs, 2018; Galbraith, 1982; Nadler & Tushman, 1980; Senge, 1994; Tichy, 1983; Weisbord, 1976), team-based work design (Cohen & Bailey, 1997; Hackman & Oldham, 1980; Mohrman, Cohen, & Mohrman, 1995), and multilevel modelling (Klein & Koslowski, 2000; Klein 1994)—specifically the micro-foundations of strategy and the resource-based view of the firm, including the role of social capital in competitive advantage (Buller & McEvoy, 2012; Burt, 1997; Leana & Van Buren, 1999; Leenders & Gabbay, 1999; Nahapiet & Ghoshal, 1998; Tsai & Ghoshal, 1998).

The objective of managing job performance is as old as human history, and it leads organisational leaders to focus on individuals. First, much work is done in isolation and appears to rely only on the individuals in the role. Second, roles are staffed, developed, and managed one person at a time. Third, each individual within a group has to do their job for the group to perform effectively; consequently, every performance management system contains a strong individually-focused element. Think about the imagery behind phrases such as 'one throat to choke' or 'the buck stops here.' Both emphasise the bias of leadership and organisational members to assign responsibility for collective efforts to individuals.

The problem is that the obsessive focus on individuals obscures critical role interdependencies. The literature on teams explicitly uses interdependence to delineate the difference between a 'true' team versus a more loose collection of individuals who are part of a group (Cohen & Bailey, 1997; Hackman & Oldham, 1980). However, even when the interdependence is looser, the concept of 'no person is an island' applies universally to every single role in an organisation, which raises a fundamental challenge to the idea of KSAs/KSAOs, competencies, and talent: how much should these reflect individual versus group issues?

One part of the answer is that competencies arose in part because there is a difference between knowing how to do something in general versus performing the work in the right way at the right time. The language of KSAs implies a static state that precedes the person applying the KSAs on the job. 'Competence' and 'talent' more directly suggest that one's KSAs are applied correctly for job and organisational performance.

The second and more relevant part of the answer is that, because jobs do not exist in a vacuum, successful performance requires that the individuals appropriately work with their team/group members and other organisational roles effectively. They have to address the interdependencies of their role with others; otherwise, performance will fall short.

Role interdependence challenges are the main reason why managerial competencies are so challenging to define and measure consistently. Managers or leaders, by design, do not do the vast majority of the work themselves; their primary responsibility is to create the conditions for others to do the work, provide feedback, and hold them accountable for performance. Consequently, it is problematic predicting how a manager will perform in a role—except by observing past performance in similar positions.

Because of the challenges of interdependence, the better competency efforts often explicitly call out how well the individual works with others. Examples include competencies such as 'achieves performance objectives the right way' (does not overwork team members, takes into account larger organisational objectives and not just what the person can directly impact, etc.) and ones that specifically focus on team-based work— such as team leadership, team/collective orientation, having shared mental models or shared understanding about the group's work and how to perform it, and trust.

The Relationship between Competencies and Performance

Competencies are a catchall for the knowledge, skills, and abilities (KSAs) needed for effective job performance. Competencies address procedural knowledge (Fantl, 2017; Ryle, 1949) and the knowledge of how to do something—which can be both explicit and tacit (Nonaka, 1994; Nonaka & von Krogh, 2009; Polanyi, 1966).

Competencies that correspond with explicit knowledge are easy to identify and typically are associated with the foundational KSAs needed to meet minimum performance standards. For example, a machine operator needs to be able to operate machinery effectively; a financial controller needs to know basic accounting principles; a nurse needs a foundation of technical medical knowledge, and so on.

KSAs that correspond to minimum performance standards are indeed competencies, yet they are not necessarily what would be included in most competency models. That is because competency models, when done well, more often focus on what differentiates performance among incumbents in a role—especially the contrast between average or slightly below average performers compared to high performers. People who fail to meet minimum performance standards either never get hired into the role or are moved out once they cannot meet the minimum standard. Consequently, samples of incumbents should have few to no people who lack the KSAs to meet the minimum requirements.

There is very little empirical evidence on the performance impacts of competencies at the individual, unit, or organisational levels. To my knowledge, only five published studies have addressed future performance impacts—performance differences that are predicted by differences in competencies—and these all focus on managerial competencies. Anecdotally, there appear to be many, many more case studies where the design and impact of competency systems have been evaluated by both internal experts and external consultants (Campion et al., 2011), yet the results have not been shared publicly in highly detailed ways nor been subject to peer review.

Spreitzer, McCall, and Mahoney (1997) found that specific competencies predicted subsequent performance ratings by supervisors. Bray, Campbell, and Grant (1974) and Dulewicz and Herbert (1999) found that competencies predicted career advancement—which implies they predicted performance though no direct link was tested. Russell (2001) showed a relationship between competencies used for the selection of general managers and the subsequent performance of their units. Levenson, Van der Stede, and Cohen (2006) found a link between competencies used for rewards for first-line and middle managers and unit performance.

Based on these results, advocates might conclude that competencies play their intended role. However, some methodological issues need to be addressed before reaching such a conclusion. First, this is a small number of studies relative to the vast amount of organisations that use competencies. The empirical evidence supports the conclusion that competencies *can* improve performance. However, the evidence neither supports nor refutes the claim that competencies *do* improve performance the way they are typically implemented in organisations.

Unfortunately, we likely will never have sufficient scientific research evidence to resolve the debate definitively. Difficulty in collecting scientifically valid data ensures that, at most, only a minimal number of competency models ever will be tested for their performance impact. An additional problem is the setting required to show a real link to organisational performance: sufficient variation in competency system characteristics (e.g., a sizeable cross-company study or significant within-organisation variation) to enable differentiation of the impacts of competency systems versus other factors including technology, organisation design, and HR systems.

Second, the results from these studies are consistent with a contingency or context-specific relationship between competencies and performance (Youndt, Snell, Dean, & Lepak, 1996). In the Spreitzer, McCall, and Mahoney (1997), Dulewicz and Herbert (1999), and Russell (2001) studies, only a subset of the competencies differentiated subsequent performance or career advancement. In the Levenson, Van der Stede, and Cohen (2006) study, there was a link between competencies and unit performance in the middle and large units but not in the small units. These results are consistent with the 'big tent' approach to building competency models—including a large number of competencies either (a) because of uncertainty regarding which competencies lead to better performance in general (a small number of competencies matter, regardless of the setting), (b) because of a desire to anticipate a range of performance scenarios requiring different sets of competencies (which competencies matter depend on the context), or (c) both.

Assuming this 'big tent' interpretation is correct, how is it best to use such far-reaching models in practice? If only a subset of competencies predict performance, is it possible to know ahead of time which ones will be indicative of future performance? Since competency models are constructed by comparing the traits of 'superior performance' incumbents with the traits of 'average performance' incumbents, then there should be a strong correlation between all identified competencies and subsequent performance when applied to a new sample, as the studies cited above tested. However, only a subset of competencies mattered or mattered only in specific settings—suggesting standard competencies identification does not have a lot of predictive validity *vis-à-vis* future performance.

This raises questions about the candidates who are screened out by a competency-based selection process. If candidates are screened based on meeting a minimum level of competence for every single competency in the model, yet only a subset of the competencies predicts future performance, then might suitable candidates be inaccurately screened out? Candidates who score low on the competencies that do not predict future performance but high on the competencies that do may be improperly excluded. This critique applies even if competencies are more predictive of job performance than intelligence or assessment tests; the argument is that the rate of false negatives (i.e., rejecting suitable applicants) is lower under a competency approach than a test approach but not equal to zero. This may be legally acceptable but not ideal for organisational performance.

Another issue is that competency requirements change over time (Hollenbeck & McCall, 2003). If the competencies are not sufficiently forward-looking, then they will not be tied closely enough to strategy and may imperfectly predict future performance. This is consistent with McCall's (1998) concern that the competencies that should matter are much more forward-looking than those that typically appear in competency models.

Competencies and Talent in Non-Managerial Work

Non-managerial competencies usually are non-controversial because they closely relate to readily-verified job requirements. For example, healthcare jobs such as being a doctor, nurse, and physician assistant all have well-defined skills that directly match job tasks, and the task performance can be readily ascertained. Examples include taking a patient's vital signs, administering diagnostic tests, interpreting test results, drawing blood, administering injections, and preliminarily diagnosing a patient's ailments, with different levels of expertise for doctors versus nurses versus physician assistants. Competencies for most non-managerial jobs have much face validity.

Reasonably strong empirical evidence of the validity of competencies for non-managerial roles comes from research on skill-based pay plans. When pay is tied to skills in non-managerial roles, there can be more significant learning and maintenance of skills (Dierdorff & Surface, 2008), with positive impacts on productivity, labour costs, and quality (Murray & Gerhart, 1998). However, the effects are most evident in manufacturing (Shaw, Gupta, Mitra, & Ledford, 2005), which represents a minority of employment in the economy. Moreover, skill-based pay plans are less likely to survive when the strategy includes technical innovation (Shaw et al., 2005).

The Shaw et al. (2005) results have important implications for understanding competency model limitations, especially for knowledge and related work where performance is hard to measure objectively. What distinguishes manufacturing from most service work is a set of clear, objective measures of performance including quality, up-time, waste, inventory cycle turns, and many more. These measures leave little to no room for interpretation: if they are met, the organisation's strategy usually is successful.

As a consequence, modern manufacturing organisations have developed sophisticated, accurate views of work design and staffing for optimal return on investment. Over decades of experimentation and refinement, manufacturing systems today are well designed with clear accountabilities for performance. In such settings, it should be no surprise that skill-based pay can have positive impacts on productivity. Thus competency models for non-managerial work in manufacturing may directly contribute to organisational performance.

Services, which account for most work in developed countries, are distinct from manufacturing. On the one hand, in industries such as retail, hotels and lodging, telecommunications, logistics, and more, there are objective measures of organisational performance that compare favourably to manufacturing. Though the validating research has not been conducted, my reading of the evidence is that competencies and skill-based pay should be able to play similarly positive roles in promoting organisational performance in these service industries.

However, in many other service industries, the ideal outcomes are much harder to specify and attain, including education, medicine, advertising, professional services (including consulting), movie production, and most industries based on internet-based technologies such as social networks. Quantifying customer value in these industries is much harder to quantify: many essential customer outcomes cannot be easily measured in real-time, requiring long time delays for validation.

In these cases, competency identification is not the problem. The challenge is validating the link between competencies and organisational performance, which is next to impossible when the organisation cannot determine with certainty in real-time how it is impacting customers. For example, the appropriate patient outcomes often are observable only for an extended time after the initial delivery of health services. Financial audit quality often can solely be determined years later, by a lack of errors emerging. Predicting the economic success of the vast majority of movies is a fool's errand. There are no universally agreed-upon measures for the quality of education. Moreover, the business model of most new internet-based technologies only emerges slowly over time as products are launched and end users engaged.

The further challenge is innovation, which changes the work and renders existing competency models irrelevant. This is why skill-based pay systems are less resilient under innovation strategies (Shaw et al., 2005). That evidence is consistent with critiques of backward-looking competency models, which most are (Hollenbeck & McCall, 2003; McCall, 1998).

Snell and Dean (1994) provide additional evidence regarding the evolution of manufacturing and the role of skill-based pay. During the second half of the 20th Century, integrated manufacturing arose, comprised of three main elements: advanced manufacturing technology, just-in-time inventory control, and total quality management (Dean & Snell, 1991). Before integrated manufacturing, the pay was set based on the work performed, not necessarily the person's skills: since task-based pay is straightforward, there was no need to complicate matters by considering skill. However, integrated manufacturing made the work much more complex, and, thus, hard to directly verify if it was performed correctly. The move towards skill-based pay was a way to link pay to changing job requirements to ensure organisational performance—and it worked (Snell & Dean, 1994).

The implication is that competencies can be directly linked to performance through pay, but the strength of the linkage depends on the context. One way to interpret the Dean and Snell (1991) and Snell and Dean (1994) results is that competency-based pay may become more important when there are greater interdependencies in the work. The results from Levenson et al. (2006) are consistent: in that case, the organisation adopted competency-based pay while moving from a command-and-control type of management that focused on performance only within the manager's direct report team, to a system that emphasised continuous learning, team-based decision-making, and interdependencies among managers at each manufacturing site.

Interdependencies were central to the quality revolution in manufacturing that W. Edwards Deming helped foster in the middle of the 20th Century (Deming, 1994; Shewhart & Deming, 1986; Walton, 1986). His work led directly to the adoption of self-managing teams and other strategies that ultimately led to integrated manufacturing. Those same interdependence principles helped propel global supply chains and just-in-time production, among other management innovations. Greater interdependencies today in service and other non-manufacturing industries imply a strong argument for competencies and competency-based pay for non-managerial roles, even if it is not always possible to make a direct link between competency models and organisational performance.

Competencies and Talent in Managerial Work

Research in the 1960s and 1970s on managerial roles and effectiveness was the precursor to competencies, including Drucker (1966), Dunnette, Campbell, Lawler, and Weick (1970), Argyris (1971), Bray, Campbell, and Grant (1974), and many more. The term 'competencies' was not used widely then—emerging in the 1980s and 1990s with the foundation laid by McClelland in the 1970s.

In the 1990s and early 2000s, there was a fairly robust debate regarding how managerial competencies should be measured (Hollenbeck & McCall, 1999, 2003; Spreitzer, McCall, & Mahoney, 1997), how they are developed (McCauley, Ruderman, Ohlott, & Morrow, 1994), and what their impact is on advancement and performance (Dulewicz & Herbert, 1999; Levenson, Van der Stede, & Cohen, 2006; McKenna, 2002; Russell, 2001). A summary of the conclusions and outstanding issues follows.

Managerial competencies are typically assessed using multisource feedback—such as 360 evaluations—which is more effective when used solely for feedback, and not for evaluation and performance management (London, 2001, 2003). However, authors such as London and others repeatedly have to remind practitioners about the limitations of multisource feedback because of the allure of using it for evaluation.

I have had to cite the evidence countless times in my work with companies globally because of the following dynamic: the feedback is introduced initially for developmental purposes and usually has a positive impact—aligning managerial behaviours with strategy—leading to perceptions that it positively contributes to organisational culture and performance. As faith in the competency system improves, senior leaders observe a reliable measurement system and mistakenly conclude it would be straightforward to hold managers accountable for the behaviours. The leaders then incorporate the ratings into the performance management system—following this, the quality of the system degrades.

When multisource feedback is incorporated into performance management, the people being rated often feel undue pressure to focus on the ratings themselves rather than the improvements in their behaviours. In today's world, corporate profitability and productivity levels are at all-time highs because organisations have gotten masterful at increasing the demands on managers—frequently creating burdensome workloads and overly ambitious performance goals. Worrying about multisource feedback affecting performance ratings and rewards diverts the needed time and energy away from focusing on the behavioural objectives.

Since behavioural ratings are subjective, there is too much arguing over the ratings at the expense of focusing on the behaviours themselves. This increases pressure to include only dimensions that can be more directly linked to current performance in the role rather than behaviours that might be important for organisational culture and the development of skills needed for performance in subsequent roles. Consequently, competency model dimensions can be much broader when used for development and talent identification and not for performance management.

Another challenge is that collecting multisource feedback can be cumbersome, as it typically happens only once per year or, at most, once per quarter. Point-in-time snapshots cannot identify when needed behaviours are context-specific—a key missing feature. For example, extraversion is strongly associated with many dimensions of job performance and career success (Wilmot, Wanberg, Kammeyer-Mueller, & Ones, 2019), and point-in-time measurements are likely to over-emphasize mean differences across managers that such behaviours over-emphasise. For example, higher marks for extroverts in multisource feedback are expected to show up in dimensions—such as the ability to communicate effectively.

However, actual managerial performance often depends as much, if not more on, when and how behaviours are applied and not just whether they are applied more often (Levenson, 2009). An extroverted manager should receive better ratings on communication skills, and those ratings, in turn, can facilitate faster and further career advancement. At any rate, what often matters more for performance is knowing when and how to apply the skills. An introverted manager can perform better by choosing strategically when to communicate more directly by selecting the situations when communication needs are at a premium, as compared to an extroverted manager who generally communicates well but fails to hit the mark in a handful of the most critical instances. Thus, while competency models can measure behaviours that matter on average, the competency evaluations cannot cost-effectively measure the nuances of effective application in context.

A related concern is important behaviours that cannot be accurately assessed using multisource feedback. For example, judgement is a key managerial competency, yet it usually cannot be accurately assessed by observing behaviours. Multisource feedback of such behaviours, therefore, cannot be reliably included in a managerial competency model.

There is an interesting divide between the ubiquity of managerial competencies in organisations versus the attention paid by researchers. Following the robust debate in the 1990s and early 2000s, there have been virtually no further substantive contributions since. At the same time, competencies have become an assumed foundation of management practice in subsequent research (Dragoni, Tesluk, Russell, & Oh, 2009; Semeijn, Van der Heijden, & Van der Lee, 2014). The most recent advancements in exploring how competencies can best contribute to organisational outcomes, and how their application should be improved have all been led by IO psychologists working in consulting and inside organisations. Unfortunately, except for a handful of cases (e.g., Bartram, 2005; Campion et al., 2011), there has been very little published research—creating a large divide between the scientific and practice communities, and little attention paid to how advances in digital talent management might impact competencies' application and usefulness.

Technology's Emerging Role in Competency Identification, Management, and Development

Technology promises interesting new ways of providing feedback and measuring what happens on the job both in terms of observed behaviours and the impacts that the person has on organisational processes.

Matching People to Jobs and Internal Opportunities—The Rise of an Internal Gig Economy

Technology can help facilitate the matching of people's current capabilities with opportunities elsewhere in the organisation. The anecdotal evidence is that the technology currently is being developed primarily to match people who already have specific competencies with the immediate needs of the organisation. These new internal platforms allow people to self-identify their competencies while allowing those in need of specific skill sets to openly advertise the opportunity.

The first examples of these platforms were one-sided and applied only to open positions: it was much easier for external job applicants to find open positions in an organisation rather than those people already working within it. Given the challenges of attracting, selecting, and retaining people with the right organisation fit (Kristof, 1996; Kristof-Brown, Zimmerman, & Johnson, 2005; Schneider, 1987), sharing such information more readily with the outside world than the internal one is very economically inefficient. Therefore, the first innovations created transparency in job postings for potential internal applicants. This helped contribute to more active internal labour markets (Bidwell, 2012; Groysberg, Lee, & Nanda, 2008) which arose through more efficient matching (Keller, 2018).

Companies with existing competency systems already have the profiles of all of the employees covered by the system, but these are not used for the systematic matching of people to roles and assignments. The second wave of innovation has been changing that by collecting all the individual competency profiles and making these available in a central database. With such a database, the organisation can more efficiently find people internally to fill open roles or work on assignments—which is what IBM did, starting in 2005. IBM developed a taxonomy of 100 job classifications and 10,000 skills in a database that internal consultants could use to look up who had the requisite skills for a task (Forelle, 2005). The company reported that this led to a decreased use of outside contractors and greater utilisation of its staff.

Such a sophisticated database and matching system makes business sense for any industry or organisation with a large, diverse set of technical skills among its core employees. Anecdotally, I have come across other organisations that have taken steps along a similar path as IBM—moving towards developing a centralised database of competency profiles. However, I sense that professional services are exceptional in the volume and churn rate of such assignments: the business model's success relies on project managers quickly assembling new teams of people to solve a potentially unlimited set of configurations of those skills for every single client engagement. Outside of professional services - where work assignments tend to evolve less rapidly—there may not be a business case that is as strong.

The third and most recent wave of innovation is so new that virtually nothing has been documented until very recently: the internal gig marketplace for projects and tasks (Goldberg & Steven-Waiss, 2020). The concept is the same as the gig marketplaces that thrive outside organisations, such as Topcoder and Upwork (Boudreau, Jesuthasan, & Creelman, 2015). The difference is that the external marketplaces are run by third parties, and for people who are external to the organisation. In contrast, the internal marketplaces are accessible only by current employees of the firm. The phenomenon seems to be at a potential tipping point, with adopters including Cisco, Patagonia, Seagate Technology, Unilever, eBay, Dolby Laboratories, HERE Technologies, Accenture, and Tata Communications (Goldberg & Steven-Waiss, 2020; Unilever, 2019).

The strength of the internal marketplace is that it can be either tightly defined, loosely defined, or both. IBM's model, as described above, is built on a firm foundation with a taxonomy of job classifications and skills. That foundation creates an efficient way to post openings and search for people with particular sets of skills. However, it is cumbersome, time-consuming, and not always accurate in carefully enumerating all of the core skills needed for a task.

A loose architecture allows the posting of opportunities with less rigorous rules on how to specify the skills. The downside is it can be hard to search for specific opportunities. Thus, it appears likely that as these systems evolve, they are likely to combine elements of both tight and loose architectures. Flexible architectures will help ensure that the taxonomies can evolve to meet emerging skill needs. When new skills appear, the postings would need to rely more on general descriptions of the work rather than selecting prespecified skills from the existing taxonomy. Over time and as more is learned about how the new skills are best employed, the skills can be codified within the more formal taxonomy system.

An additional advantage of internal marketplaces is that they can incorporate ratings of how a person performed the work. Such ratings are common in external marketplaces, but there is no enforcement mechanism to ensure that ratings are given accurately every time. With internal marketplaces, the system operators can require ratings with enforcement through explicit sanctions or via cultural pressure. Such enforcement mechanisms are not feasible for external marketplaces where the financial motives for the system operator are to make money from maximising the volume of matches.

The quality of ratings on internal marketplaces also has the potential to be much higher than external markets, because everyone works for the same organisation. No one would want to be responsible for promoting someone's work on a project if it would negatively impact future similar work on other projects for the same organisation. Sanctioning to ensure quality ratings is viable in an internal marketplace and is largely infeasible on external marketplaces.

Competency Identification and Development

When competency systems were first developed in the 1980s and 1990s, the processes were mostly manual, and data were not collected centrally for analysis. The focus was on determining whether job incumbents possessed the predefined competencies that were set ahead of time. Recent technological developments have improved how competencies are applied and analysed.

As technology advanced, online forms made it easier for individuals to self-identify competencies that did not fit into predefined categories. This enabled richer conversations regarding their developmental objectives, job performance, and career advancement. Organisations simultaneously have been increasing their HR analytics capabilities (Edwards & Edwards, 2019; Guenole, Ferrar, & Feinzig, 2017; Kahn & Millner, 2020; Levenson, 2015). This has led to increased insights on internal career paths and how people's competencies contribute to organisational success.

For example, organisations can now produce detailed mappings of people's experiences working in different roles and projects over extended periods of time. These can be linked to measures of project success—providing insights into correlations between work experience, competencies, organisational performance and career success. While it can be hard to establish valid causal links between competencies and performance (Levenson et al., 2006), being able to show statistical relationships between competencies and performance is an improvement over the alternative of using only performance ratings.

The problem with using performance ratings to differentiate how people contribute to organisational performance is two-fold. First, there is the halo effect: subjective performance ratings can be artificially inflated by positive organisational performance outcomes that are not due to the person's efforts and deflated by adverse outcomes beyond their control. Since competencies are evaluated separately from performance, then these should be less susceptible to performance-related halo effects.

The second problem with performance ratings is range restriction and minimal variation. Performance ratings usually vary only along a minimal 1 to 4, 1 to 5, or 1 to 10 scale and are unidimensional. Competencies, in contrast, are multidimensional. Each competency dimension usually is rated on a similarly limited 1 to 4 scale. However, since there are multiple competencies, there is much more considerable between-person variation in competency ratings. This enables more rich analyses of competencies and performance that provide more useful guidance rather than analysing only performance ratings.

Automating and Expanding the Scope of Competency Evaluation—For Managers

Assessing individual behaviours or competencies using multisource feedback such as 360 (or 270 or 180) evaluations is infinitely more practical today with the evolution of online tools. Advances in technology have enabled fully automated competency rating systems that take information electronically and quickly provide customised manager-specific reports.

It is just as important to note that there have been recent technological advances that provide new windows on managerial behaviours and impacts. This should help move how competencies are used in organisations to a more balanced approach that embodies more learning and feedback and less measurement and control—if done right.

For example, recent technology advances enable linking employee survey responses to individualised feedback reports by manager, so they can see how their team members feel about their leadership, engagement, intention to turnover, career satisfaction, and more. Pulse surveys and advanced reporting engines enable real-time feedback on how organisational initiatives are unfolding, so managers can course-correct in real-time. The new tools include natural language processing of open-ended survey questions to provide a much quicker turnaround while highlighting key themes that might have otherwise been missed.

New technology tools also enable easier linking of individual competencies with team performance data. This is an important advancement because of the challenges of effectively measuring performance at the individual level when performance in most settings is more of an interdependent group phenomenon (Levenson, 2018). Though such linkage analysis is not causal, the results provide rich feedback to managers and team members about the correlations of performance. The managers and team members can then use team-based problem solving to build the capability needed to achieve and maintain high performance.

Another innovation is organisational network analysis (ONA). ONA is a social science research method that enables the mapping of the 'informal organisation'—key influencers and enablers of decision-making and change who are not formally identified in the organisation charts of roles and responsibilities (Cross & Thomas, 2008; Johnson-Cramer, Parise, & Cross, 2007; Parise, Cross & Davenport, 2006). ONA has been around for a long time in the social science research community. Recent advances in technology and internal analytics capability have greatly increased the opportunity to apply ONA using both traditional approaches such as asking employees directly with whom they interact as well as using the 'digital exhaust' and Big Data' solutions (Neef, 2014) that analyse patterns of electronic communications using 'relationship analytics.'

For competency evaluation, ONA is best suited to analyse the competencies of people who show up as being more influential or able to drive change. Leaders usually have a strong point of view regarding the behaviours they want to encourage and enable. ONA can help either validate the importance of those behaviours or reveal other behaviours and individual characteristics that may be more important for organisational performance.

A Few Words on COVID-19

Here is a final note regarding the massive economic disruptions caused by the COVID-19 coronavirus. Organisations and individuals have had to make a sudden shift towards doing large amounts of work virtually, wherein these were previously conducted entirely face-to-face (FTF; Levenson, 2020). The disruptions to FTF work have required the use of digital tools and interfaces in ways that push the boundaries of effective teaming and collaboration (Levenson & McLaughlin, 2020). This sudden shifting of work will provide new insights into the strengths and weaknesses of digital tools and platforms for enhancing productivity which, in turn, will inform the evolution of competency models to increase future productivity.

Competency Models and the Future of Work

Recent technological advancements have made it more cost-effective to collect and analyse data about competencies and the linkage between competencies and performance. However, these do not address why people act the way they do and what should be done to improve this.

For example, Microsoft's new office productivity tools—which are a type of individualised-ONA—provide nudges to managers regarding team members who may need additional feedback without telling them how to better provide feedback. The tools could be counterproductive if treated as a check-the-box exercise: the system's requirements can be satisfied through meaningless communication that does not improve communication, feedback, or transparency.

As an alternative, consider how ONA is applied more traditionally. Identifying critical players in the system that others turn to is a significant first step. However, what is the best way to leverage that information? Should they be promoted to a higher-level role or left in place? Should they be given greater rewards and recognition to honour their contributions, or are they intrinsically motivated to do the work? Should their work be redesigned to free them up, so they can be even more impactful day-to-day? If so, how: should they be put on more cross-functional teams, invited to key meetings, given greater decision-making authority, consulted on key organisational initiatives, etc.? Technological advancements can provide deeper insights into the role of competencies in corporate performance, but those insights are usually only the starting point of more in-depth inquiries needed to improve performance.

An additional area that remains under-addressed is the role of interdependencies in the workplace. Competency models for individual contributors have been mainly treated as tools for feedback and development at the individual level. The models can include team-focused behaviours such as being a team player, supporting team members when they need help, etc. However, focusing on how the individual contributes to the team can obscure how interdependent work is actually conducted.

Consider two different types of teamwork—one that includes loose interdependencies among group members and another that works on tight interdependence. An example of the former is a group of automobile salespeople in a dealership; for the latter, an example is a cross-functional new product development team in pharmaceuticals. A competency model for each could easily include the dimensions of 'provides timely support to teammates when they need it' and 'works to ensure that levels of trust are established and maintained at work.'

The work of the new product development team is highly interdependent, because if any member does not do their part, then the team will fail. Each member's contributions have to be closely aligned and coordinated with one another to avoid inefficiencies, time delays, and poor decision-making. In contrast, individual auto salespeople can successfully do their work without substantial coordination with one another. They have to work effectively—and interdependently—with other people in the dealership who handle the paperwork, financing, closing details, etc., but that coordination is mainly sequential—a handoff from the salesperson to the next person in the sales process. The coordination on the new product development team, in contrast, has to happen in a highly synchronised fashion with little room for error.

These two examples help highlight the gap in most competency models: team-level dynamics that are key for performance. Evolving competency models to reflect effective teaming requires integrating them into other organizational development and change processes—which is not standard practice. Recent technological advancements can support an integrated approach such as using surveys, giving rapid feedback of results, and alerting people within the organisation who can help improve team dynamics.

References

Argyris, C., (1971). *Management and organisational development: The path from XA to YB*. New York: McGraw-Hill.

Bartram, D., (2005). The great eight competencies: A criterion-centric approach to validation. *Journal of Applied Psychology*, *90*(6), 1185–1203.

Bidwell, M., (2012). Paying more to get less: The effects of external hiring versus internal mobility. *Administrative Science Quarterly*, *56*(3), 369–407.

Boudreau, J. W., Jesuthasan, R. & Creelman, D., (2015). *Lead the work: Navigating a world beyond employment*. San Francisco: Jossey-Bass.

Bray, D. W., Campbell, R. J. & Grant, D. L., (1974). *Formative years in business: A long-term AT&T study of managerial lives*. New York: John Wiley & Sons.

Buller, P. F. & McEvoy, G. M., (2012). Strategy, human resource management and performance: Sharpening line of sight. *Human Resource Management Review*, *22*, 43–56.

Burke, W. W. & Litwin, G. H., (1992). A causal model of organisational performance and change. *Journal of Management*, *18*(3), 523–545.

Burt, R. S., (1997). The contingent value of social capital. *Administrative Sciences Quarterly*, *42*(2), 339–365.

Campion, M. A., Fink, A. A., Ruggeberg, B. J., Carr, L., Phillips, G. M. & Odman, R. B., (2011). Doing competencies well: Best practices in competency modeling. *Personnel Psychology*, *64*, 225–262.

Cohen, S. & Bailey, C., (1997). What makes teams work: Group effectiveness research from the shop floor to the executive suite. *Journal of Management*, *23*(3), 239–290.

Cross, R. & Thomas, R. J., (2008). How top talent uses networks and where rising stars get trapped. *Organisational Dynamics*, *37*(2), 165–180.

Dean, J. W. & Snell, S. A., (1991). Integrated manufacturing and job design: Moderating effects of organisational inertia. *Academy of Management Journal*, *34*(4), 776–804.

Deming, W. E., (1994). *The new economics for industry, government, education*. Cambridge, MA: Massachusetts Institute of Technology.

Dierdorff, E. C. & Surface, E. A., (2008). If you pay for skills, will they learn? Skill change and maintenance under a skill-based pay system. *Journal of Management*, *34*(4), 721–743.

Dierdorff, E. C. & Wilson, M. A., (2003). A meta-analysis of job analysis reliability. *Journal of Applied Psychology*, *88*(4), 635–646.

Dragoni, L., Tesluk, P. E., Russell, J. E. A. & Oh, I. S., (2009). Understanding managerial development: Integrating developmental assignments, learning orientation, and access to developmental opportunities in predicting managerial competencies. *Academy of Management Journal*, *52*(4), 731–743.

Drucker, P. F., (1966). *The effective executive*. New York: Harper & Row Publishers.

Dulewicz, V. & Herbert, P., (1999). Predicting advancement to senior management from competencies and personality data: A seven-year follow-up study. *British Journal of Management*, *10*, 13–22.

Dunnette, M. D., Campbell, J. P., Lawler, E. E. & Weick, K. E., (1970). *Managerial behavior, performance and effectiveness.* New York: McGraw-Hill.

Edwards, M. & Edwards, K., (2019). *Predictive HR analytics: Mastering the HR metric,* 2nd Edition. Kogan Page.

Falletta, S. & Combs, W., (2018). The organisational intelligence model in context: A comparative analysis and case profile. *OD Practitioner, 50*(1), 22–29.

Fantl, J., (2017). Knowledge How, *The Stanford Encyclopedia of Philosophy* (Fall 2017 Edition), Zalta, Edward N. (ed.), Retrieved from https://plato. stanford.edu/archives/fall2017/entries/knowledge-how.

Federal Register. (1978). *Part 1607 - uniform guidelines on employee selection procedures (1978), United States federal government Title 29 - Labor. Subtitle B - Regulations relating to labor (continued.), Equal Employment Opportunity Commission, 4,* 2011–07. https://www.govinfo.gov/content/pkg/ CFR-2011-title29-vol4/xml/CFR-2011-title29-vol4-part1607.xml.

Forelle, C., (2005). IBM tool dispatches employees efficiently. *Wall Street Journal,* 14 July 2005. Retrieved from www.wsj.com/articles/SB112130518499485395.

Galbraith, J. R., (1982). Designing the innovating organisation. *Organisational Dynamics, 10,* 4–25.

Ghiselli, E. E., (1973). The validity of aptitude tests in personnel selection. *Personnel Psychology, 26,* 461–477.

Goldberg, E. & Steven-Waiss, K., (2020). *The inside gig: How sharing untapped talent across boundaries unleashes organisational capacity.* LifeTree Media.

Groysberg, B., Lee, L. & Nanda, A., (2008). Can they take it with them? The portability of star knowledge workers' performance. *Management Science, 54*:7, 1213–1230.

Guenole, N., Ferrar, J. & Feinzig, S., (2017). *The power of people: Learn how successful organisations use workforce analytics to improve business performance,* FT Press.

Hackman, J. R. & Oldham, G. R., (1980). *Work redesign.* Reading, MA: Addison-Wesley.

Hollenbeck, G. P. & McCall, M. W. Jr., (1999). Leadership development: Contemporary practices. In Kraut, A. I. & Korman, A. K. (Eds.). *Evolving practices in human resource management.* San Francisco: Jossey-Bass Publishers, 172–200.

Hollenbeck, G. P. & McCall, M. W. Jr., (2003). Competence, not competencies: Making global executive development work. In Mobley, W. H. & Dorfman, P. W. (Eds.). *Advances in global leadership.* Oxford: Elsevier Science Ltd., *3,* 101–119.

Hogan, J. & Holland, B., (2003). Using theory to evaluate personality and job-performance relations: A socioanalytic perspective, *Journal of Applied Psychology, 88*(1), 100–112.

Hunter, J. E. & Hunter, R. F., (1984). Validity and utility of alternative predictors of job performance, *Psychological Bulletin, 96*(1), 72–98.

Johnson-Cramer, M. E., Parise, S. & Cross, R. L., (2007). Managing change through networks and values, *California Management Review*, *49*(3), 85–109.

Kahn, N. & Millner, D., (2020). *Introduction to people analytics: A practical guide to data-driven HR*, Kogan Page.

Keller, J. R., (2018). Posting and slotting: How hiring processes shape the quality of hire and compensation in internal labour markets, *Administrative Science Quarterly*, *63*(4), 848–878.

Kerr, S., (1975). On the folly of rewarding A, while hoping for B, *Academy of Management Journal*, *18*(4), 769–783.

Kitson, H. D., (1921). Scientific method in job analysis, *Journal of Political Economy*, *29*(6), 508–516.

Klein, K. J., Dansereau, F. & Hall, R. J., (1994). Levels issues in theory development, data collection, and analysis. *Academy of Management Review*, *19*(2), 195–229.

Klein, K. J. & Koslowski, S. W. J. (Eds.). (2000). *Multilevel theory, research, and methods in organisations*. San Francisco, CA: Jossey-Bass/Wiley.

Kristof, A. L., (1996). Person-organisation fit: An integrative review of its conceptualisations, measurement, and implications, *Personnel Psychology*, *49*(1), 1–49.

Kristof-Brown, A. L., Zimmerman, R. D. & Johnson, E. C., (2005). Consequences of individuals' fit at work: A meta-analysis of person-job, person-organisation, person-group, and person-supervisor fit, *Personnel Psychology*, *58*(2), 281–342.

Lawler, E. E., (2000). *Rewarding excellence: Pay strategies for the new economy*. San Francisco: Jossey-Bass.

Leana, C. R. & Van Buren, H. J. III. (1999). Organisational social capital and employment practices. *Academy of Management Review*, *24*(3), 538–555.

Leenders, R. T. A. J. & Gabbay, S. M., (1999). *Corporate social capital and liability*. Boston, MA: Kluwer Academic.

Levenson, A., (2009). Measuring and maximising the business impact of executive coaching, *Consulting Psychology Journal*, *61*(2), 103–121.

Levenson, A., (2015). *Strategic analytics: Advancing strategy execution and organisational effectiveness*, San Francisco: Berrett-Koehler.

Levenson, A., (2018). Using workforce analytics to improve strategy execution, *Human Resource Management*, *57*, 685–700.

Levenson, A., (2020). A long time until the economic new normal, *Sloan Management Review*, April 10 2020. Retrieved from https://sloanreview.mit.edu/article/a-long-time-until-the-economic-new-normal.

Levenson, A. & McLaughlin, P., (2020). New leadership challenges for the virtual world of work, *Sloan Management Review*, 4 June 2020. Retrieved from https://sloanreview.mit.edu/article/new-leadership-challenges-for-the-virtual-world-of-work/.

Levenson, A., Van der Stede, W. & Cohen, S., (2006). Measuring the relationship between managerial competencies and performance, *Journal of Management*, *32*(3), 360–380, 2006.

London, M., (2001). The great debate: Should multisource feedback be used for administration or development only? In Bracken, D. W., Timmreck, C. W. & Church, A. H. (Eds.), *The handbook of multisource feedback: The comprehensive resource for designing and implementing MSF processes*, 368–385. San Francisco: Jossey-Bass.

London, M., (2003). *Job feedback: Giving, seeking, and using feedback for performance improvement*, Second Edition, Mahwah, NJ: Lawrence Erlbaum Associates.

McCall, M. W., Jr. (1998). *High flyers: Developing the next generation of leaders.* Boston, MA: Harvard Business School Press.

McCauley, C. D., Ruderman, M. N., Ohlott, P. J. & Morrow, J. E., (1994). Assessing the developmental components of managerial jobs, *Journal of Applied Psychology, 79*(4), 544–560.

McClelland, D. C., (1973). Testing for competence rather than for 'intelligence.' *American Psychologist, 28*: 1–14.

McClelland, D. C., Baldwin, A. L., Bronfenbrenner, U. & Strodtbeck, F. L., (1958). *Talent and society.* Princeton: Van Nostrand.

McKenna, S., (2002). Can knowledge of the characteristics of 'high performers' be generalised? *Journal of Management Development, 21*: 680–701.

Michaels, E., Handfield-Jones, H. & Axelrod, B., (2001). *The War for Talent.* Boston: Harvard Business Review Press.

Mohrman, S. A., Cohen, S. G. & Mohrman, A. M., (1995). *Designing team-based organisations: New forms for knowledge work.* San Francisco: Jossey-Bass.

Munsterberg, H., (1913). *Psychology and industrial efficiency.* Boston: Houghton Mifflin.

Murray, B. & Gerhart, B., (1998). An empirical analysis of a skill-based pay program and plant performance outcomes. *Academy of Management Journal, 41*(1), 68–78.

Nadler, D. A. & Tushman, M. L., (1980). A model for diagnosing organisational behavior, *Organisational Dynamics, 8*, 35–51.

Nahapiet, J. & Ghoshal, S., (1998). Social capital, intellectual capital, and the organisational advantage. *Academy of Management Review, 23*(2), 242–266.

Neef, D., (2014). *Digital exhaust: What everyone should know about big data, digitisation and digitally driven innovation*, Pearson FT Press.

Nonaka, I., (1994). A dynamic theory of organisational knowledge creation, *Organisation Science, 5*(1), 14–37.

Nonaka, I. & von Krogh, G., (2009). Tacit knowledge and knowledge conversion: Controversy and advancement in organisational knowledge creation, *Organisation Science, 20*(3), 635–652.

Parise, S., Cross, R. & Davenport, T. H., (2006). Strategies for preventing a knowledge-loss crisis, *Sloan Management Review, 47*(4), 31–38.

Polanyi, M., (1966). *The tacit dimension*, London: Routledge & Kegan Paul.

Reilly, R. R. & Chao, G. T., (1982). Validity and fairness of some alternative employee selection procedures, *Personnel Psychology, 35*, 1–62.

Russell, C. J., (2001). A longitudinal study of top-level executive performance. *Journal of Applied Psychology, 86*: 560–573.

Ryle, G., (1949). *The concept of mind.* Chicago: The University of Chicago Press.

Schmitt, N., Gooding, R. Z., Noe, R. A. & Kirsch, M., (1984). Metaanalyses of validity studies published between 1964 and 1982 and the investigation of study characteristics. *Personnel Psychology, 37,* 407–422.

Schneider, B., (1987). The people make the place. *Personnel Psychology, 40,* 437–453.

Schneider, B. & Konz, A. M., (1989). Strategic job analysis. *Human Resource Management, 28*(1), 51–63.

Semeijn, J. H., Van der Heijden, B. I. J. M. & Van der Lee, A., (2014). Multisource ratings of managerial competencies and their predictive value for managerial and organisational effectiveness. *Human Resource Management, 53*(5), 773–794.

Senge, P. M., (1994). *The fifth discipline: The art & practice of the learning organisation.* New York: Doubleday Business.

Shaw, J. D., Gupta, N., Mitra, A. & Ledford, G. E., (2005). Success and survival of skill-based pay plans. *Journal of Management, 31*(1), 28–49.

Shewhart, W. A. & Deming, W. E., (1986). *Statistical method from the viewpoint of quality control.* Mineola, NY: Dover Publications.

Shippman, J. S., Ash, R. A., Battista, M., Carr, L., Eyde, L. D., Hesketh, B., Kehoe, J., Pearlman, K., Prien, E. P. & Sanchez, J. I., (2000). The practice of competency modeling. *Personnel Psychology, 53*(3), 703–740.

Snell, S. A. & Dean, J. W. Jr. (1994). Strategic compensation for integrated manufacturing: The moderating effects of jobs and organisational inertia. *Academy of Management Journal, 37*(5), 1109–1140.

Spencer, L. M., Jr. & Spencer, S. M., (1993). *Competence at work: Models for superior performance.* New York: John Wiley & Sons, Inc.

Spreitzer, G. M., McCall, M. W. Jr. & Mahoney, J. D., (1997). Early identification of international executive potential. *Journal of Applied Psychology, 82,* 6–29.

Tichy, N. M., (1983). *Managing strategic change: Technical, political, and cultural dynamics.* New York: John Wiley & Sons.

Tsai, W. & Ghoshal, S., (1998). Social capital and value creation: The role of intrafirm networks. *Academy of Management Journal, 41*(4), 464–476.

Unilever, (2019). Unilever launches new AI powered talent marketplace. 28 June 2019. Retrieved from www.webwire.com/ViewPressRel_print.asp?aId=242981.

Walton, M., (1986). *The Deming management method.* New York: The Berkeley Publishing Group.

Weisbord, M., (1976). Organisational diagnosis: Six places to look for trouble with or without a theory. *Group & Organisation Studies, 1,* 430–447.

Wiblen, S. & Marler, J. H., (2020). The human-technology interface in talent management and the implications for HRM, HRM 4.0 For Human-Centered Organisations, *Advanced Series in Management, 23,* 99–116.

Wilmot, M. P., Wanberg, C. R., Kammeyer-Mueller, J. D. & Ones, D. S., (2019). Extraversion advantages at work: A quantitative review and synthesis of meta-analytic evidence. *Journal of Applied Psychology, 104*(12), 1447–1470.

Youndt, M. A., Snell, S. A., Dean, J. W. Jr. & Lepak, D. P., (1996). Human resource management, manufacturing strategy, and firm performance. *Academy of Management Journal, 39*, 836–866.

Zerga, J. E., (1943). Job analysis: A resume and bibliography. *Journal of Applied Psychology, 27*, 249–267.

Zingheim, P., Ledford, G. E. Jr. & Schuster, J., (1996). Competencies and competency models: One size fits all? *ACA Journal, 5*(1), 56–65.

5 People Analytics Maturity and Talent Management

Linking Talent Management to Organisational Performance

Janet H. Marler and Lexy Martin

If We Could Say One Thing:
Advancements in information technology applied to people analytics now enable organisations to more convincingly document how talent management may be linked to financial performance.
—Janet H. Marler and Lexy Martin

Introduction

Numerous case studies in the business press and white papers assert a positive relationship between human resource management (HRM) practices and organisational performance. While many arguments—such as strategic alignment of HRM with business strategy and automating HRM processes with information technology to free HR managers for more strategic tasks—are well known, much of the evidence is sponsored by consultants and suppliers of digital HRM. As such, they tend to be biased toward promoting a product or service, and few measure financial performance outcomes such as increased profitability, return on assets, or total shareholder return. There is, however, also a growing body of scientific research that supports the more general relationship between strategic HRM and firm financial performance (Delery & Roumpi, 2017; Jiang & Messersmith, 2018; Marler, 2012). However, does this link also apply to talent management? Scholars are searching for valid and reliable evidence concerning this question, and managers want to know to take effective action. This is where people analytics plays a role.

In this chapter, we report on a recent scientific study that includes measures of financial performance, talent management, and people analytics maturity and the evidence linking all three. We begin by defining talent management and people analytics. We then review the literature on value chains that serves as the basis for linking people analytics, information technology, and talent management to organisational performance. Drawing on this foundation, we propose a model, which we call the *People Analytics Talent Management Value Chain*. We test our model with data collected from managers who participated in a survey conducted by a people analytics technology supplier. We conclude the chapter with implications and recommendations for managers.

Defining Talent Management

Although talent management is sometimes confounded with HRM or strategic human resources management (SHRM), scholars have been careful to distinguish it as separate and distinct. In this chapter, we use Cappelli and Keller's (2014) definition of talent management (TM) as 'the process through which organisations meet their needs for talent in strategic jobs.' In this definition, talent management is distinguished from HRM in that it applies only to a segment of the organisation's workforce. Not every employee is considered 'talent' and as such talent management is exclusive, not inclusive. In this regard, Cappelli and Keller (2014) further define talent as individuals who currently or have the potential to differentially contribute to firm performance by occupying strategic jobs, now or in the future. Second, talent management focuses on both talented individuals and strategic jobs. More specifically, talent management involves first identifying strategic jobs in the organisation and then identifying individuals who can perform best in those jobs. Not only does an individual have to be talented but this individual must also be matched to a strategic job.

A key assumption underlying the growth of interest in talent management is that effective talent management is a leading indicator of organisational performance. Collings (2014) points out, however, a key limitation in the research on talent management is that 'There is very limited empirical evidence of the link between talent and performance.' Addressing this gap, Collings (2014) emphasises the importance of identifying strategic jobs or key positions. These jobs are comprised of two elements. First, these involve executing the organisation's strategic goals, and second, the variance in performance of these jobs by the people who perform them must be substantial such that talented individuals make a difference in strategically important outcomes (Becker & Huselid, 2006; Boudreau & Ramstad, 2007; Cappelli & Keller, 2014; Collings, Mellahi, & Cascio, 2019).

A second critical aspect of TM is creating 'talent pools.' Thus, rather than succession planning for specific jobs, talent management involves developing pools of talented individuals with competencies that are useful across a range of roles rather than one specific job. In this way, an organisation has slack human capital that allows it to accommodate better dynamic product and labour market conditions (Cappelli, 2008; Collings, 2014).

Third, talent management involves differentiating the bundle of human resource management practices to ensure that the talent pool is properly linked and embedded in strategic positions across the organisation. This involves creating a customised high-performance work system just to create and manage identified organisational talent.

What continues to be lacking in the scholarly literature on talent management, however, is empirical evidence concerning the validity of proposed models. There still exists minimal data to test whether the relationship between these recommended approaches to talent management makes a difference. This is where information technology, data, and people analytics have a role to play because, in combination, these make it possible to collect and analyse the data necessary for validating this relationship.

Defining People Analytics

Data analytics in HRM followed the emergence of the digital economy and Big Data. Initially termed 'workforce analytics,' other labels followed including HR analytics, talent analytics, predictive HR analytics, and people analytics—the latter emerging as the most frequently used term (Edwards & Edwards, 2019; Marler & Boudreau, 2017; Tursunbayeva, Di Lauro, & Pagliari, 2018). Along with different names, there are differing definitions. These definitions and labels have several things in common, however (Marler, Cronemberger, & Tao, 2017). First, people analytics does not focus exclusively on human resource management (HRM) functional data. Instead, it involves linking data from other internal functions as well as data external to the firm. Second, people analytics involves using information technology to digitise, store, manipulate, report, and visualise data. Third, people analytics is about supporting people-related decisions. Finally, people analytics is about linking HRM decisions to employee, operational, and organisational outcomes. Thus, while traditional HR metrics such as headcount, administrative cost per employee, and percent participation in employee training programs, along with descriptive satisfaction survey data, are useful, these do not provide insights into the real impact of HR programs and practices on organisational and employee outcomes (Lawler, Levenson, & Boudreau, 2004). People analytics, therefore, significantly expands on the more functionally narrow descriptive insights that HR metrics provide decision-makers.

Bringing various definitions together, we define people analytics as:

> *an information technology-enabled process that meets the need for evidence-based decision-making information through identifying or establishing statistically validated direct, indirect, and contingent relationships with HR processes, social and human capital, employee outcomes, other business processes, and outcomes to organisational performance.*

Our definition is useful to the study and consideration of Digitalised Talent Management, because it highlights the role of information technology and the importance of establishing the impact on organisational performance.

Value Chains and People Analytics

Explanations about how people analytics links HRM to operational and financial outcomes are rooted in various theoretical models. The first model—known as the LAMP model (Boudreau & Ramstad, 2007)—stands for the interrelationship of logic, analytics, measures, and processes that is key to developing a cause-effect model that predicts the relationship between HRM processes and business outcomes. As summarised in their book *Investing in People*, Cascio and Boudreau (2011) explain that 'logic' provides the story behind the connections between the numbers and the causes and effects. 'Measures' represent how the outcomes of HRM are quantified. 'Analyses' are the statistical methods used to find the answers in the data, and 'process' represents how the connections and insights from logic, analysis, and measurement are used in the organisation to improve outcomes. Cascio and Boudreau argue that the LAMP framework is 'a useful logical system for understanding how measurements drive decisions, organisation effectiveness and strategic success.'

In addition to the LAMP model, the HR Scorecard is another model that establishes how HRM and people are linked to business outcomes (Becker, Ulrich, & Huselid, 2001). The HR Scorecard is based on the Balanced Scorecard (Kaplan & Norton, 2007), which integrated the literature on total quality management and the employees' role in continuously improving processes with the literature on financial economics, which emphasised financial performance as the best measure of maximising shareholder value (Kaplan & Norton, 2007). In creating the Balanced Scorecard, Kaplan and Norton (2007) underscored how employee and process performance are critical for current and future success. The key was to have a measurement and management system that included both operational metrics as leading indicators and financial metrics as lagging outcomes to measure a company's progress in driving future performance. Another key feature of the Balanced Scorecard is its focus on strategy implementation. Strategy implementation is achieved by linking customer, operational processes, and learning and growth metrics to the ultimate organisational objective, financial performance.

Managers make predictions concerning how operational outcomes are linked to financial outcomes in a series of cause-and-effect (input to output) propositions. The first cause-and-effect relationships implied by this model are that higher employee engagement (leading indicator and HRM process outcome) is linked to better operational/internal business process quality and productivity (an internal business process outcome). The second cause-and-effect relationship in the model predicts that better process quality and process productivity result in superior product delivery (operational outcome). The third cause-and-effect hypothesis is that improved product delivery causes more customer loyalty (customer outcome). Finally, the last cause-and-effect prediction is that greater customer loyalty causes a higher return on assets (financial performance).

Kaplan and Norton's Balanced Scorecard, introduced in 1992, is also similar to and developed in parallel with the service management profit chain (Heskett, Jones, Loveman, Sasser Jr, & Schlesinger, 1994, 2008; Kaplan, 2009) which is the third model in people analytics literature. The service management profit chain links internal service quality—such as state-of-art information systems and trained customer-facing employees—to employee satisfaction. Employee satisfaction is linked to employee loyalty which, in turn, is linked to external service value. External service value—such as how insurance providers provide fast and easy claims processing—enhances customer satisfaction. Customer satisfaction promotes customer loyalty which improves organisational profitability (see Heskett et al., 1994). This value chain model, first published in 1994, has been one of *Harvard Business Review's* most successful and most cited articles (e.g., Editor's Note in Heskett et al., 2008). In a recent scholarly publication, Hong, Liao, Hu, and Jiang (2013) summarised the empirical evidence on testing this value chain. Their meta-analysis provides convincing evidence that HRM practices are leading indicators of financial outcomes working indirectly through service climate, employee attitudes, behaviours, and customer satisfaction.

A key challenge in most organisations is to derive these value chains. To do this, managers who have in-depth knowledge of their operational processes need to think about their processes in terms of inputs or drivers that cause value-added outcomes or effects. These value-adding processes should link to the ultimate outcome, financial performance. Kaplan and Norton call this the strategy mapping process. Strategy mapping is a value-chain creation process that links outcomes from employee, operational, and customer processes to financial results. Managers make predictions concerning how operational outcomes are linked to financial outcomes in a series of cause-and-effect (input-to-outcome) propositions. Pulling all of these hypothesised relationships together results in a value chain in which a human resource outcome is a strategic driver or leading indicator that indirectly, *over time* and through intervening operational outcomes, results in an effect on financial outcomes (Marler & Fisher, 2017). Financial outcomes are considered lagging indicators, because they occur after or because of earlier strategic actions.

Once a value chain model is developed, it must be validated. This is where people analytics plays a key role. Are the goals achieved, and do the cause and effect relationships hold? To do this, the organisation must develop a system of metrics—a people analytics scorecard that shows how HR actions are linked to financial outcomes. In their book, *the HR Scorecard*, Becker, Huselid, and Ulrich (2001) call attention to key metric Strategic HR Deliverables. Strategic HR deliverables are HR drivers that serve to execute the firm's strategy. There are two types of Strategic HR Deliverables: HR performance drivers and HR performance enablers. HR performance drivers are HR outcomes that can be indirectly linked to financial outcomes. For example, Quantum, a leading manufacturer of storage devices determined that their ability to ramp up new product innovations to deliver to customers on a timely basis was a critical capability that, ultimately, was related to sales volume. In developing their value chain model, Quantum identified a set of value behaviours such as taking the initiative for one's development, and resolving complaints and issues in an objective manner that were related to the timely ramp-up of new products. In this example, the HR performance drivers that needed to be measured were the value behaviours because they were indirectly linked to sales volume through their relationship with the timely ramp-up of new products. An HR performance enabler reinforces HR performance drivers. In this example, an HR performance enabler would be training programs that supported the development of value behaviours. The measurement of this performance enabler would be the satisfaction with this training program or performance score on a test given after completion of the training program.

People Analytics and Talent Management Value Chain

Building on this foundational research on value chains, we developed a People Analytics Talent Management Value Chain. Depicted in Figure 5.1, we propose that people analytics and talent management represent HR performance drivers with employee engagement as an HR enabler. These HR performance drivers and enablers predict financial outcomes. In our model, the operational outcome is employee productivity. The financial outcomes are profit margin and return on assets—both regarded as key indicators of organisational financial health and return on investors' capital.

People Analytics and Information Technology

Laying the foundation for people analytics and fuelling its adoption is the company's vast storage of electronic data that is collected by its information technology system and the increasing availability of technological innovations, such as business intelligence tools and reporting tools including dashboards and scorecards. To meet the rising demand for easily accessible information for decision-making, software vendors have developed software solutions that integrate business software applications with broad reporting and analysis functionality. These software solutions are generally called Corporate Performance Management (CPM) or Enterprise Performance Management (EPM)

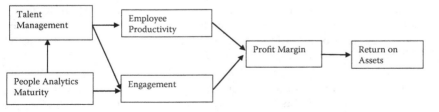

Figure 5.1 People Analytics Maturity and Talent Management Value Chain.

(Ohata & Kumar, 2012). EPM systems must integrate different sources of data such as transactional data from different functions (e.g., financial, supply chain, customer, and human resources), unstructured data (e.g., written text in social media or employee surveys), and data from external suppliers (e.g., salary survey data, benefits data). These data need to be stored in data repositories which may include data warehouses or data lakes and then easily retrieved to produce information.

The retrieved information must be communicated in useful ways that are either configured into electronic or printed standard and ad hoc reports and finally into 'dashboards' and 'scorecards.' The diffusion of this technological capability is still at an early stage, given the complexity and expense of implementation. However, as software vendors continue to innovate, companies will have more options and the accessibility to increasingly sophisticated reporting and analytical capabilities.

The key to transforming data into information for decision-making is in integrating the capabilities of the information technology with the capabilities of the company's managers who will be using the technology to access information to make decisions. In the next section, we describe how this might be accomplished.

People Analytics Maturity

Several applied practitioner research studies indicate that data-driven organisations outperform on various financial metrics (for example, see, studies by Bersin by Deloitte, SierraCedar, and Visier Inc.). In a Visier study, a key finding was that people analytics technology adoption, with associated people analytics maturity characteristics, was indirectly related to improved business results through improved HR and talent outcomes (Martin, 2018). As depicted in Figure 5.2 taken from the Visier Inc. study authored by Martin, organisations do not just adopt a technology solution and immediately improve financial value. Instead, successful organisations adopt solutions, evolve their practices, and improve their HR/talent and business outcomes, and this, in turn, improves financial metrics. Figure 5.2 illustrates the basic concept of an HRM value chain which is based on the Balanced Scorecard and service-profit chain discussed earlier.

A key concept in Figure 5.2 is People Analytics Maturity, which comes from adopting people analytics solutions where more solutions indicate higher sophistication and more advanced process maturity. Maturity also comes from more and broader user types, as well as more data sources, enabling organisations to both impact and realise

Figure 5.2 People Analytics Value Chain Model: Linking People Analytics to HR and Business Outcomes to Financial Value.

business outcomes. A culture of change management and practices further contributes to the successful implementation of people analytics. Hypothesised to be an HR performance driver of profit margin and return on assets, People Analytics Maturity is measured by the People Analytics Maturity Index (PAMI). PAMI is a sum of counts and scores of how people analytics are performed, the types of users, the role of data in decision-making, data sources, partners for success, and the degree and extent of change management used in an organisation. The components of the PAMI are shown in Figure 5.3 (again from Martin's authored Visier report).

Validating the People Analytics Talent Management Value Chain

To validate our proposed talent management value chain shown in Figure 5.1, we used survey data from The Age of People Analytics Survey (Martin, 2018) and structural equation modelling (SEM) analyses. SEM path analyses enabled us to determine whether our proposed strategic HR drivers—People Analytics Maturity and Talent Management—were indirectly and statistically significantly related to financial performance outcomes across a large sample of organisations located primarily in North America.

The survey[1] was conducted over the last quarter of 2017 and the first quarter of 2018 and targeted organisations with single-source respondents who were familiar with people analytics and had at least 500 employees. The final useable sample consisted of 259 organisations

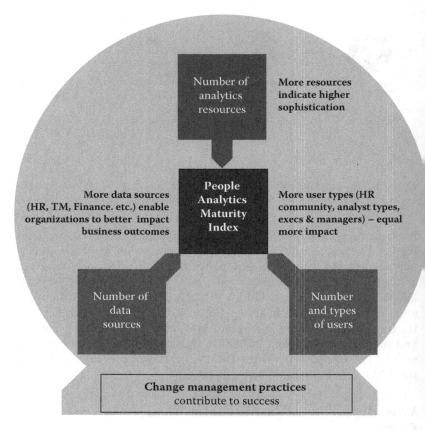

Figure 5.3 People Analytics Maturity Index.
(Source: The Age of People Analytics: Survey on Characteristics, Value Achieved, and Proven Practices of Successful Organisations: https://www.visier.com/wp-content/uploads/2018/06/The-Age-of-People-Analytics-Survey-Report.pdf).

that were primarily medium-sized (less than 10,000 employees) and from the high-technology, manufacturing, financial services, and healthcare industries. Out of these 259 organisations, a subsample of 45 was publicly traded and, therefore, could be matched with financial data collected from Compustat. Data to construct measures used in the structural equation model (SEM) were derived from quantitatively scaled responses to survey questions and to sales, net income, and total assets that financial data collected separately for each survey respondent organisation. Thus, the first HR driver in the model, the People Analytics Maturity Index was measured as described above and illustrated in Figure 5.3, as the sum of count data from questions on how people analytics are performed, the number of user types, the role of data in decision-making, the level of people analytics process maturity, the number of data sources, the number of partners for success, and the degree of change management. For example, for the question on how people analytics are performed, respondents could select from a list of six that included spreadsheets, reports, or analytics included in our HRMS, the use of dedicated people analytics solution, the use of own data discovery and statistical analysis tools, the use of business intelligence and data warehouse, and others. The highest score for this item comprising the People Analytics Maturity Index (PAMI) was 6. With 7 similar items comprising the PAMI, a respondent's score could range from 7 to 49.

The second HR driver—talent management—was measured using a multi-item scaled response to the survey question, 'Over the past year, how have the following HR outcomes changed across your organisation?'. The response choices to this question were quantitatively scored with a choice of 1 to 5, in which 1 = significantly declined, 3 = unchanged, and 5 = significantly improved. The choices of HR outcomes included eights items: (1) ability to attract top talent, (2) ability to develop a highly qualified workforce, (3) availability of workforce data for decision-making, (4) employee and management productivity, (5) HR alignment with business strategy, (6) cost-efficiency, (7) retention of top or key employees, and (8) talent management (attraction, development, and retention). Our measure of talent management comprised of the summed-up scale scores of 5 of these items—ability to attract top talent, ability to develop a highly qualified workforce, HR alignment with business strategy, retention of top or key employees, and talent management (attraction, development, and retention). The alpha reliability for this measure is .80, representing strong reliability.

We measured two HR enablers—employee engagement and employee productivity—with one-item measures. For employee engagement, we created our measure from the respondent's response to the question, 'Over the past year, how have the following business outcomes changed across your organisation?' The business outcomes included a scaled response to several items—including competitive advantage, cost efficiency, customer satisfaction, employee engagement, innovation, and market share. We used the scaled response from 1 to 5 for employee engagement, where 1 = declined significantly, 3 = no change, and 5 = improved significantly.

For employee productivity, we created our measure from the respondent's response to the question, 'Over the past year, how have the following HR outcomes changed across your organisation?'. This question comprised of eight items: (1) ability to attract top talent, (2) ability to develop a highly qualified workforce, (3) availability of workforce data for decision-making, (4) employee and management productivity, (5) HR alignment with business strategy, (6) cost-efficiency, (7) retention of top or key employees, and (8) talent management (attraction, development, retention). We used the scaled response from 1 to 5 for employee and management productivity, where 1 = declined significantly, 3 = no change, and 5 = improved significantly.

We included two financial measures—profit margin and return on assets. Profit margin measures the profits generated annually from operations and is calculated as net income/sales. Return on assets (ROA) measures the return that business assets generate for investors and is calculated as net income/total assets.

Descriptive statistics are reported in Table 5.1. Organisations in this sample, on average, have good profit margins —an average of 15%—and return on assets —an average of 9%. The average response for talent management, employee engagement, and employee productivity also indicates respondents reported, on average, a modest improvement over the past year. Also, both talent management and employee engagement are significantly and positively correlated with ROA, and PAMI is correlated with employee engagement directly but not with any of the financial performance measures. We now discuss the results of our analyses in which we look for indirect relationships between PAMI and financial performance through its relationship with employee engagement as an HR enabler.

Table 5.1 Means, Standard Deviation, and Correlations of Study Variables

		Mean	*SD*	*1*	*2*	*3*	*4*	*5*
1	PAMI	21.74	6.40					
2	Talent Management	17.38	2.20	0.22				
3	Employee Engagement	3.32	0.71	**0.33**	**0.54**			
4	Employee Productivity	3.36	0.54	0.13	**0.58**	**0.33**		
5	Profit Margin	0.15	0.14	0.22	0.32	**0.46**	**0.45**	
6	ROA	0.09	0.08	0.06	**0.40**	**0.57**	0.31	**0.69**

$n = 37$ bolded coefficients are significant at $p < .05$.

Table 5.2 Structural Equation Model Path Analysis Direct, Indirect, and Total Effects

	Effect Variables														
	Talent Management			Employee Engagement			Employee Productivity			Profit Margin			Return on Assets		
Driver Variables	Unst	SE	p	Unst	SE	p	Unst	SE	p	Unst	SE	p	Unst	SE	p
PAMI															
Direct effect	0.09	0.06	—	0.032	0.016	*	—	—	—	—	—	—	—	—	—
Indirect effect	—	—	—	0.013	0.009	—	0.012	0.008	—	0.005	0.003	*	0.003	0.001	*
Total effect	0.09	0.06	—	0.047	0.018	**	0.012	0.008	—	0.005	0.003	*	0.003	0.001	*
Talent Management															
Direct effect	—	—	—	0.150	0.040	***	0.140	0.033	***	—	—	—	—	—	—
Indirect effect	—	—	—	—	—	—	—	—	—	0.028	0.008	***	0.015	0.004	***
Total effect	—	—	—	0.150	0.040	***	0.140	0.033	***	0.028	0.008	***	0.015	0.004	***
Employee Engagement															
Direct effect	—	—	—	—	—	—	—	—	—	0.090	0.028	***	—	—	—
Indirect effect	—	—	—	—	—	—	—	—	—	—	—	—	0.048	0.018	**
Total effect	—	—	—	—	—	—	—	—	—	0.090	0.028	***	0.048	0.018	**

(Continued)

Table 5.2 (Continued)

	Effect Variables														
	Talent Management			Employee Engagement			Employee Productivity			Profit Margin			Return on Assets		
Driver Variables	Unst	SE	p	Unst	SE	p	Unst	SE	p	Unst	SE	p	Unst	SE	p
Employee Productivity															
Direct effect	–	–	–	–	–	–	–	–	–	0.112	0.044	**	–	–	–
Indirect effect	–	–	–	–	–	–	–	–	–	–	–	–	0.059	0.020	**
Total effect	–	–	–	–	–	–	–	–	–	0.112	0.044	**	0.059	0.020	**
Profit Margin															
Direct effect	–	–	–	–	–	–	–	–	–	–	–	–	0.530	0.120	***
Indirect effect	–	–	–	–	–	–	–	–	–	–	–	–	–	–	–
Total effect	–	–	–	–	–	–	–	–	–	–	–	–	0.530	0.120	***

Using SEM and sample measures, we tested the fit of our proposed path analysis SEM model shown in Figure 5.1, in which we expect PAMI and Talent Management to be indirectly related to financial performance. Our results reported in Tables 5.1 and 5.2 indicate that the sample data fit the model well, thus, meeting the first step in statistically validating our model. The fit statistics indicate a well-fitting model with CFI = .94, TLI = .87, and SRMR = .05 and a chi-square statistic with 7 degrees of freedom equal to 11.9—which is not significantly different from the proposed model (p = .13). All fit statistical values are within acceptable fit ranges (Kline, 2005).

These results, thus, indicate that PAMI and talent management are both significantly and indirectly related to financial performance through improved employee engagement and employee productivity. Using the parameters shown in Table 5.2, a one-unit increase in PAMI is associated with about a 3% increase in return on assets and a 4% increase in profit margin. A 10% improvement in PAMI would be associated with about a 7% increase in return on assets and an 8% increase in profit margin. Our results also show that a 10% improved change in talent management is associated with a 7% increase in return on assets and an 8% increase in profit margin.

Using structural equation modelling, our proposed value chain shows that people analytics adoption and maturity are significantly and indirectly related to profit margins and return on assets. Based on these preliminary statistical results, we, therefore, estimate that increasing components of PAMI are associated with an increased return on assets. These components include:

- Increasing people analytics solutions,
- Increasing the number of user types (from not only analytics personnel and HR roles, but also to business leaders and managers),
- Increasing the number of data sources used in the analytics solutions and going beyond just including HR and talent management data, and also including financial and operational data sources that can more clearly connect workforce performance to business performance, and
- Improving change management practices and moving beyond just training and communications to practices such as creating a vision that includes moving to a data-driven culture, creating a network of HR business partners and upskilling them to evangelise people analytics, and establishing a centre of excellence focused on providing workforce insights.

Connecting People Analytics and Talent Management: Real Case Examples

Recent case studies also confirm the relevance of this survey-based statistical evidence. For example, a client of a people analytics technology solution provider—a high-tech product organisation, analysed various team factors against various outcome factors to determine if they could predict the best mix of team members to achieve better team performance. To do this, they explored various characteristics of teams in marketing, product development, and customer service and also collected data on business development opportunities, revenue, and customer satisfaction, respectively. For the analysis of the teams, the firm looked at the manager, manager span of control, promotability, productivity (revenue per team member), engagement scores (at team level only), and quality of hire. By creating a team index, they could see which teams were most closely aligned with business outcomes and then discovered how to configure teams to achieve the highest outcomes in terms of business development opportunities, revenue, and customer satisfaction.

In another example illustrating the importance of integrating people analytics, information technology, and talent management at a bio-pharmaceutical firm, attracting talent was very challenging because qualified candidates had their pick of many other high-tech firms as well. This firm found that by getting granular in analysing its processes for attracting, developing, and retaining the workforce, there were weaknesses in how they managed diversity. By focusing on the diversity mix and whether there was unconscious bias in the attracting and interviewing of candidates, they were able to increase diverse hiring. By focusing on development opportunities of diverse employees, they were able to ensure inclusion in promotion opportunities. They were also able to look at employee engagement scores to see that diverse workforce pools felt equitably treated and stayed, thereby improving retention.

What is Next for Academics and Business Professionals?

Many organisations that have set up people analytics efforts or are in the process of evaluating whether or not to do so are interested in whether there truly is value in doing so. Case stories help. ROI models using data from vendors that have enough success among their customers can be used to forecast potential savings or revenue. However, a more rigorous approach to measuring value, as suggested here, will be of interest to the people analytics practitioners community. After all, they use analytics to improve workforce decisions, so why not also use analytics to evaluate their success? To do this, organisations must realise the need to increase their level of people analytics maturity.

Practitioners can also evaluate the value chain model illustrated here and customise it according to their organisation. They can begin by identifying strategic HR drivers and HR enablers. Next, they can identify all business groups that report to a manager who has the responsibility for measurable financial or operational outcomes. Next, they can start collecting data from employees on HR drivers, HR enablers, and business group-level financial and operational outcomes. They can pull in financial metrics associated with the line of business of the managers and employees. Rather than use ROA and profit margin that are single organisational metrics, they can bring in revenue and/or profit numbers by the line of business. Having the right data is critical for using people analytics to establish links between talent management and performance.

Finally, practitioners need to evaluate whether they have data analytic competencies in their organisation or if they need to partner with academic researchers or data analytic consultants to test their value chain models using structural equation modelling.

Conclusion

When the case study and survey analyses are considered together, in this chapter, we have provided compelling evidence that shows that organisations strong in people analytics and talent management have stronger financial performance than other organisations. These relationships are not direct but are, rather, indirect through a chain of value-adding outcomes. People analytics maturity and talent management are linked to and enabled by employee engagement—which is associated with better profit margins and return on assets. Also, talent management is linked to and enabled by employee productivity—which is also associated with better profit margins and return on assets. What is next is further studies that either validate or invalidate the results found here. Such additional research would build on the results we provide in this chapter and, thus, continue to provide more detailed guidance and meaningful support for future managerial decision-making related to effective people analytics and talent management.

Note

1   For a complete description of the survey and data gathering process see 'The Age of People Analytics: Survey on Characteristics, Value Achieved, and Leading Practices of Advanced Organisations' (https://www.visier.com/wp-content/uploads/2018/06/The-Age-of-People-Analytics-Survey-Report.pdf retrieved June, 2019) written by Lexy Martin, Principal Research and Customer Value for Visier Inc.

References

Becker, B. E., & Huselid, M. A. (2006). Strategic human resources management: Where do we go from here? *Journal of Management, 32*(6), 898–925.

Becker, B. E., Ulrich, D., & Huselid, M. A. (2001). *The HR scorecard: Linking people, strategy, and performance* (1st edition). Harvard Business Review Press.

Boudreau, J. W., & Ramstad, P. M. (2007). *Beyond HR: The new science of human capital*. Boston, MA: Harvard Business School Publications.

Cappelli, P. (2008). *Talent on demand: Managing talent in an age of uncertainty*. Boston, MA: Harvard Business Press.

Cappelli, P., & Keller, J. (2014). talent management: Conceptual approaches and practical challenges. *Annual Review of Organisational Psychology and Organisational Behavior, 1*(1), 305–331.

Cascio, W., & Boudreau, J. (2011). *Investing in people: The financial impact of human resource initiatives* (2nd edition). Upper Saddle, NJ: Person Press.

Collings, D. G. (2014). The contribution of talent management to organisation success. In *The Wiley Blackwell handbook of the psychology of training, development, and performance improvement* (pp. 247–260). John Wiley & Sons, Ltd.

Collings, D. G., Mellahi, K., & Cascio, W. F. (2019). Global talent management and performance in multinational enterprises: A multilevel perspective. *Journal of Management, 45*(2), 540–566.

Delery, J. E., & Roumpi, D. (2017). Strategic human resource management, human capital and competitive advantage: Is the field going in circles? *Human Resource Management Journal, 27*(1), 1–21.

Edwards, M. R., & Edwards, K. (2019). *Predictive HR analytics: Mastering the HR metric* (2nd edition). New York: Kogan Page Ltd.

Heskett, J. L., Jones, T. O., Loveman, G. W., Sasser Jr., W. E., & Schlesinger, L. A. (1994). Putting the service-profit chain to work. *Harvard Business Review, 72*(2), 164–170.

Heskett, J. L., Jones, T. O., Loveman, G. W., Sasser Jr., W. E., & Schlesinger, L. A. (2008). Putting the service-profit chain to work. *Harvard Business Review, 86*(7/8), 118–129.

Hong, Y., Liao, H., Hu, J., & Jiang, K. (2013). Missing link in the service profit chain: A meta-analytic review of the antecedents, consequences, and moderators of service climate. *Journal of Applied Psychology, 98*(2), 237–267.

Jiang, K., & Messersmith, J. (2018). On the shoulders of giants: A meta-review of strategic human resource management. *International Journal of Human Resource Management, 29*(1), 6–33.

Kaplan, R. S. (2009). Conceptual foundations of the balanced scorecard. In Chapman, C. & Shields, M. (Eds.), *Handbook of management accounting research* (Vol. 3). Elsevier Science.

Kaplan, R. S., & Norton, D. P. (2007). Using the balanced scorecard as a strategic management system. *Harvard Business Review, 85*(7/8), 150–161.

Kline, R. B. (2005). *Principles and practice of structural equation modeling* (2nd edition). New York, NY: Guilford Press.

Lawler, E., Levenson, A., & Boudreau, J. W. (2004). HR metrics and analytics: Use and impact. *Human Resource Planning, 27*(4), 27–35.

Marler, J. H. (2012). Strategic human resource management in context: A historical and global perspective. *Academy of Management Perspectives, 26*(2), 6–11.

Marler, J. H., & Boudreau, J. W. (2017). An evidence-based review of HR analytics. *The International Journal of Human Resource Management, 28*(1), 3–26.

Marler, J., Cronemberger, F., & Tao, M. (2017). HR analytics: The influence of eHRMin Talent Management. Here to stay or short-lived management fashion? In T. Bondarouk, E. Parry, & H. Ruel (Eds.). *EHRM in the Smart Era* (59–86). London: Emerald Press.

Marler, J. H., & Fisher, S. L. (2017). *Making human resource management information technology decisions: A strategic perspective.* New York: Business Expert Press.

Martin, L. (2018). *The age of people analytics: Survey on characteristics, value achieved, and leading practices of advanced organisations.* Retrieved from Visier Inc. website https://www.visier.com/wp-content/uploads/2018/06/The-Age-of-People-Analytics-Survey-Report.pdf.

Ohata, M., & Kumar, A. (2012). Big data: A boon to business intelligence. *Financial Executive, 28*(7), 63–64.

Tursunbayeva, A., Di Lauro, S., & Pagliari, C. (2018). People analytics-A scoping review of conceptual boundaries and value propositions. *International Journal of Information Management, 43*, 224–247.

6 Talent Management in the Gig Economy

A Multilevel Framework Highlighting How Customers and Online Reviews are Key for Talent Identification

Jeroen Meijerink

If I Could Say One Thing:
To understand talent identification in the gig economy, we need to understand customer reviewing behaviour and adopt a multilevel perspective on review system design, customer attributes, and gig worker performance.

—Jeroen Meijerink

Introduction: HRM Practices in the Gig Economy

Online labour platforms such as Uber, Deliveroo, and Amazon Mechanical Turk delegate a variety of human resource management (HRM) activities to consumers using digital technologies (Cassady, Fisher, & Olsen, 2018; Duggan, Sherman, Carbery, & McDonnell, 2019; Ellmer & Reichel, 2018; Kuhn & Maleki, 2017; Meijerink & Keegan, 2019). Operating in the so-called gig economy, online labour platforms do not employ workers. Instead, they matchmake between gig workers (i.e., independent contractors/freelancers) and consumers who request an on-demand service (e.g., a taxi ride, delivery of a meal, or programming of software codes) (Aloisi, 2016; Stanford, 2017; Wood, Graham, Lehdonvirta, & Hjorth, 2019). This way of working creates tensions, as online labour platforms seek to control gig workers by means of HRM activities while simultaneously disavowing they are employers (Friedman, 2014; Kuhn & Maleki, 2017; Meijerink & Keegan, 2019). To resolve these tensions, online labour platforms require consumers to enact HRM responsibilities on their behalf to ensure gig worker efforts are controlled (Meijerink, Keegan, & Bondarouk, 2019).

HRM practices within the gig economy afford customers a significant role in deciding which online gig workers are 'valuable.' Academics and practitioners alike debate the salience attributed to 'customers' and the associated customer enacted HRM responsibility. Operating within HRM practices resides *performance appraisal* (Kuhn & Maleki, 2017; Lehdonvirta, Kässi, Hjorth, Barnard, & Graham, 2018; Rosenblat, Levy, Barocas, & Hwang, 2017). In the gig economy, consumers appraise the performance of 'gig workers'—i.e., individual freelancers who offer their services to clients through an online labour platform—by leaving online reviews through five-star rating schemes or leaving a thumbs up/thumbs down after a transaction is completed. While very few would argue that online reviews are synonymous with 'talent identification,' evaluating an individual's 'performance' in a binary 'thumbs up/thumbs down' and posting comments from previous customers can influence future customers' perceptions of that individual in ways that previous performance review 'scores' shape future expectations. As such, through leaving and inquiring online reviews, consumers play a key role in deciding upon a gig worker's value and thus, who is seen as a talent.

Delegating performance appraisal responsibilities to consumers can have severe consequences for gig workers and their ability to be deemed as valuable within their specific online platform. Online reviewing by consumers is shown to impact gig workers' access to the online labour platform (Lee, Kusbit, Metsky, & Dabbish, 2015; Rosenblat et al., 2017), influences the fees which gig workers can charge for their freelance services (Lehdonvirta et al., 2018), and/or creates anxiety among gig workers (Rosenblat, 2018). Given the influential role of online appraisals on financial outcomes, talent identification, and careers, it is important and suitable to explore why consumers do or do not leave reviews. The goal of this chapter is to outline a conceptual framework on the drivers that explain why consumers engage in online appraisal in the gig economy. In developing this model, I depart from the notion that online labour platforms are nested arrangements of workers, consumers, and platform firms (Jacobides, Cennamo, & Gawer, 2018; Meijerink & Keegan, 2019). Accordingly, this chapter draws on multilevel theory (Klein & Kozlowski, 2000; Renkema, Meijerink, & Bondarouk, 2017) to (1) identify the levels at which online appraisal/reviewing by consumers and its antecedents manifest and to (2) propose a set of future research questions on why consumers do or do not leave reviews on online labour platforms. Ultimately, adopting multilevel theory enhances our understanding of why customers leave online reviews on online labour platforms and, thus, how talent identification in the gig economy takes place.

The chapter is organised as follows. I start off by discussing the gig economy, the online labour platforms and the role of consumers in identifying the value/talent of gig workers. This is followed by a discussion of why customer reviews play an essential role in talent identification in the gig economy and on online labour platforms. I conclude by outlining a multilevel framework on why customers do or do not leave online reviews and discuss implications of this framework for academics and practitioners.

Talent Management in the Gig Economy and Online Platforms

Although an agreed-upon definition of the gig economy is lacking, it is generally referred to as an economic system in which freelance 'gig workers' and customers engage in transactions which are intermediated by online labour platforms (Duggan et al., 2019; Meijerink & Keegan, 2019; Wood et al., 2019). Platform-enabled gig work is the key economic exchange which takes place in the gig economy and can be defined as the performance of fixed-term activities through an online platform by individuals (i.e., gig workers) for an individual consumer or an organisation—without being actually employed (Aloisi, 2016; Daskalova, 2018; Kuhn & Maleki, 2017; Meijerink & Keegan, 2019; Stanford, 2017). Instead, gig workers are freelancers who obtain work assignments (i.e., 'gigs') through intermediary platforms firms such as Deliveroo, Uber, or Amazon Mechanical Turk. These intermediary platform firms develop and maintain online labour platforms for matchmaking between gig workers and those who request their services in industries such as transportation (e.g., Uber), cleaning (e.g., Helpling), household do-it-yourself (e.g., TaskRabbit) and programming (e.g., Clickworker). As noted by Duggan et al. (2019), the platform-enabled gig work taking place in these industries can be classified into three groups: *capital platform work* where individuals use a platform to lease assets (e.g., Airbnb), *crowdwork* where workers remotely complete online tasks that are allocated to them through an online platform (e.g., Clickworker) and *app-work* which involves platform-intermediated tasks taking place locally (e.g., Uber).

Technology plays an important role in the operation of online labour platforms and, thus, in the rise of the gig economy. Most notably, intermediary platform firms rely on the internet and related technologies for matchmaking between supply and demand for labour. To do so, the intermediary platform develops algorithms that assign gig workers to requesters, while web/smartphone interfaces (e.g., mobile 'apps') allow customers to recruit and select gig workers

(Duggan et al., 2019; Ellmer & Reichel, 2018; Kuhn & Maleki, 2017). Beyond these mere operational activities, intermediary platform firms also rely on technology to implement a range of HRM activities. These include the use of algorithms to determine gig worker *compensation* (e.g., surge pricing by Uber where rates automatically increase when demand surges), *dismissal* where gig workers are, sometimes temporarily, automatically denied access to the online platform in case their performance falls below a certain threshold, or *workforce planning* where algorithms predict the number of gig workers needed during selected time slots (Duggan et al., 2019; Meijerink et al., 2019; Rosenblat, 2018; Wood et al., 2019).

Seen from a talent management perspective, the rise of the gig economy not only implies an increase in the use of technology for talent management purposes (such as talent attraction, selection, and retention), but it also suggests an inclusive approach towards talent management (Meyers & van Woerkom, 2014). In essence, by enacting their intermediary role, platform firms establish talent pools (Collings & Mellahi, 2009), which gig workers—as freelancers—are free to join and from which customers can recruit workers. It is in the interest of both the platform firms and the customers to be inclusive in providing gig workers access to the virtual talent pool of platform firms, as this creates network effects. Here, network effects emerge when an increase in the number of users of an online labour platform (i.e., both gig workers and customers) leads to a direct increase in value for all users (Gawer & Cusumano, 2002; Jacobides et al., 2018; Parker & Van Alstyne, 2005). For customers, an inclusive approach towards talent management in the gig economy is beneficial, as it allows them to more easily recruit gig workers that match their unique needs and wishes.

Moreover, being inclusive is useful for intermediary platform firms, as it enables them to capture value from network effects. Namely, network effects imply more exchanges between gig workers and the requesters from which the platform firm can capture a fee and which ultimately enables growth and, in some cases, market dominance (Gawer & Cusumano, 2002). Given the desire for intermediary platform firms to create network effects, it should not come as a surprise that they open their doors for new gig workers without much selection taking place (Meijerink et al., 2019; Rosenblat, 2018). As an example, Uber claims to foster maximum inclusivity and seeks to lower the (legal) barriers for gig workers in entering its online platform. Although an inclusive approach to talent management may seem apparent at a first glance, a closer look into the usage and workings of online appraisal systems on online labour platforms shows that the gig economy is not necessarily all that inclusive altogether.

Why Studying Appraisal on Online Labour Platforms is Important

At first sight, performance appraisal by consumers in the gig economy may appear to be a straightforward HRM activity. Upon the completion of a transaction via an online labour platform, consumers are presented with an online rating scale with the question to evaluate the gig worker that served them. Through a single tap on a smartphone, the appraisal of a gig worker can take just a second. While customers may think that the process is quick and easy, the evaluation inputted and processed by the embedded algorithms influences work allocation/job security and fosters an exclusive approach to talent management.

Research shows that consumers do not always leave an online review. As an example, more than a third of the transactions taking place via the Airbnb platform are left unevaluated (Fradkin, Grewal, & Holtz, 2018). In other online platforms, such as eBay, these statistics are similar and show that only 67% of platform-mediated transactions are evaluated (Dellarocas & Wood, 2008). The reasons for this need to be understood, because the availability of consumer reviews and lack thereof can have consequences for gig workers as well as consumers. First, research has shown that gig workers are 'deactivated' (i.e., dismissed in traditional HRM terms)—meaning they lose access to the online platform and, thus, generate no income when consumer evaluations fall below a certain threshold. For instance, the accounts of Uber drivers are deactivated when their average evaluation falls below a 4.6 rating on a scale from 1 to 5 (Rosenblat et al., 2017). From a talent management perspective, gig workers are excluded from a platform firm's talent pool in case their average customer evaluations fall behind. This becomes problematic when dissatisfied consumers leave reviews more often than satisfied consumers do—in particular, when a gig worker recently joins the online labour platform (Teubner & Glaser, 2018).

Secondly, an online appraisal by consumers introduces power asymmetries between gig workers and consumers (Newlands, Lutz, & Fieseler, 2018; Rosenblat & Stark, 2016). For instance, the risk of deactivation forces gig workers to spend money and other resources to offer additional services (e.g., Uber drivers providing free drinks to passengers) in hopes of inducing consumers to leave a (positive) review. This is out of line with the idea that online rating schemes are designed to reduce moral hazard. That is, gig workers and their consumers wish to transact without knowing if the transaction can be trusted by each party. Online reviews play a key role here in establishing trust among 'strangers' that want to engage in transactions (Pavlou & Gefen, 2004). Besides facilitating trust-building, rating schemes also make gig workers unnecessarily dependent on the evaluation of consumers (Rosenblat & Stark, 2016). Customer reviews further increase levels of power asymmetries between workers and consumers when online labour platforms require gig workers to evaluate customers. Namely, platform firms use gig worker-generated reviews for expelling consumers when consumers violate the rules and regulations set by the platform firm. Gig workers, however, say that they are anxious to discipline consumers that misbehave and refrain from leaving a negative review, because they are afraid that consumers might take revenge on them by leaving a negative review (Rosenblat, 2018). Such negative reviews may include customers reporting how dissatisfied they were with a gig worker's performance, recommendations to future customers to not hire the selected gig worker, or, simply leaving a one-star rating or a thumbs down score.

Finally, an online appraisal by consumers may introduce all sorts of (new) biases related to the identification and (e)valuation of talents. A well-documented bias refers to the so-called 'reputation inflation,' which occurs when available customer reviews are always positive, regardless of the actual performance of a gig worker (Dellarocas & Wood, 2008; Horton & Golden, 2015). Reputation inflation is, thus, a result of satisfied consumers leaving positive online reviews more often than dissatisfied consumers—which inflates the performance appraisal scores of gig workers. Available evidence suggests that reputation inflation is omnipresent in the gig economy by highlighting that customer reviews on online (labour) platforms are heavily skewed towards positive ratings (Dellarocas & Wood, 2008; Fradkin et al., 2018; Horton & Golden, 2015; Teubner & Glaser, 2018; Zervas, Proserpio, & Byers, 2015). Research has shown that the online reputation of gig workers is positively related to the hourly rate that gig workers charge to consumers (Lehdonvirta et al., 2018). Taken together, this suggests that reputation inflation has undesirable consequences for consumers as they end up paying higher fees to gig workers which are not justified based on the actual levels of gig worker performance. Seen from a talent management perspective, this implies that gig workers are overvalued—meaning that the majority of gig workers are wrongfully classified as 'talented.'

In conclusion, online reviews by consumers of online labour

platforms have significant implications for both gig workers, consumers, and the process of talent identification. Therefore, an important question is: why do consumers do or do not leave an online review after being served by a gig worker? Besides the technical design of online appraisal systems, many antecedents of online reviewing by consumers can be considered—such as customer satisfaction (Horton & Golden, 2015; Meijerink & Schoenmakers, 2020), incentive schemes implemented by the platform (Fradkin et al., 2018; Teubner & Glaser, 2018), the online reputation of the gig worker (Lee & Lee, 2012), consumer personality traits (Mowen, Park, & Zablah, 2007), gig worker behaviour (Rosenblat, 2018), etc. The sheer number of antecedents that are at play and that explain why consumers leave online reviews, requires a unifying framework that pulls together these antecedents into meaningful clusters. As such, the purpose of this chapter is not to provide an exhaustive list of antecedents, but instead offer a framework that highlights the vast array of factors that influences talent management in the gig economy. This is important for academic research, as the framework can be used in future studies for creating a complete overview and classification of antecedents of online appraisal by consumers in the gig economy. The framework is also useful for practitioners who wish to engage with gig workers, as it offers insights into how customers can be induced to leave online reviews and which factors can be considered to improve the workings of online review systems in the gig economy. The following section presents this framework.

Towards a Multilevel Framework of Online Consumer Appraisal

Introducing Multilevel Theory: Why Online Customer Reviews Are Multilevel

The framework presented draws on multilevel theory. Multilevel theory departs from the notion that social systems of individuals, groups, and institutions are nested arrangements. In HRM research, a multilevel theory is often applied to understand that HRM activities reside on and relate to outcomes on multiple levels of analysis—such as the organisation, team, and individual employee levels (Renkema et al., 2017). A multilevel theory presents different principles on how, where, when, and why multilevel relationships occur and, thus, constitute the fundamental theoretical building blocks that allow us to conceptualise multilevel research models (Klein & Kozlowski, 2000).

Adopting multilevel theory for understanding why consumers do or do not leave online reviews is essential, because online appraisal by customers manifests on different levels of analysis, namely the transactional level, consumer-level, and platform level (see Figure 6.1). The lowest level at which customer appraisal can be observed is the transaction level where consumers evaluate the transaction with a gig worker. At this level, variance in the online appraisal, thus, manifests in terms of whether a consumer did or did not leave an online review after engaging with a gig worker. All reviews of these transactions by an individual consumer aggregate to the second level on which online appraisal manifests—that is, the consumer level. Primarily, on the consumer level, variance occurs in terms of the percentage of transactions that an individual consumer did evaluate during a selected time frame. This is what Dellarocas and Narayan (2006) refer to as *review propensity,* which is defined as the ratio between the total number of transactions reviewed by an individual consumer during a given time period over the total number of transactions the consumer has engaged in during the same period.

Finally, variance in online appraisal manifests on the platform level in terms of the aggregate of the review propensity of all consumers active on a selected online labour platform. On this level, an online appraisal by consumers can be conceptualised as *review density,* that is, the total number of transactions reviewed by all consumers of an online platform during a given time over the total number of transactions that took place on the online platform during the same period (Dellarocas & Narayan, 2006).

Clustering the Antecedents of Online Appraisal on Three Levels of Analysis

To better understand why customers leave online reviews and, thus, how talent identification and evaluation takes place within the gig economy, I propose to consider various factors at three levels of analysis: the transaction level (one which relevant worker attributes reside), the customer level, and the platform level (see Figure 6.1). As noted by Meijerink and Keegan (2019), the implementation of HRM activities in the gig economy is contingent on the attributes and the actions of the platform firm, consumers, and workers. In line with this, I propose that online appraisal by consumers, as a form of HRM implementation, is contingent on the attributes and actions of the very same three actors. The three actors form a hierarchical/multilevel structure with workers being 'nested in' consumers (as an individual

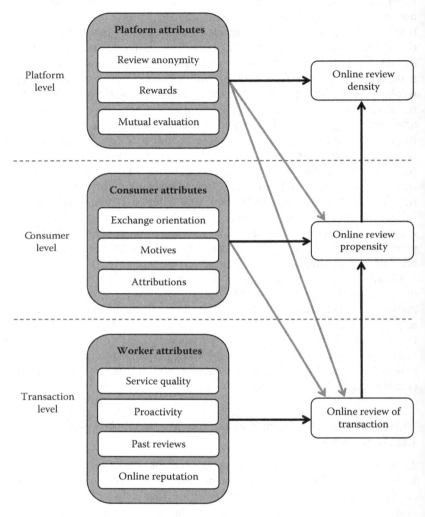

Figure 6.1 Multilevel Framework of Online Appraisal by Consumers of Online Labour Platforms.

consumer is/can be served by multiple workers) and consumers being nested in online labour platforms (i.e., as an individual platform allows a pool of consumers to engage in transactions with workers). These three levels equate the levels on which the online appraisal concepts manifest—making the worker, consumer, and platform levels useful categories for clustering the antecedents that explain why customers do or do not leave reviews on online labour platforms. Below, each level/ cluster is discussed in terms of how the attributes and actions of the platform, customer, and worker play a role in explaining online appraisal by consumers of online labour platforms.

Transaction-Level Antecedents

A vital antecedent to online appraisal is the level of (perceived) performance or service quality provided by a gig worker (Dellarocas & Wood, 2008; Meijerink & Schoenmakers, 2020). The primary goal of online appraisal by consumers is to assess the performance of gig workers. Intuitively, one might expect consumers to leave an online review when a gig worker offers either an excellent or inferior service. Research, however, shows that this is not necessarily the case in online (labour) platform settings. For instance, Dellarocas and Wood (2008) found that consumers are more likely to leave an online review when satisfied rather than when dissatisfied with a service. In line with this, Meijerink and Schoenmakers (2020) report a positive relationship between consumer perceptions of service quality and online reviewing on Airbnb, which implies that satisfied consumers are more likely to leave an online review than dissatisfied consumers.

Second, gig workers may be proactive in eliciting online reviews from consumers. Researchers, for instance, showed that Uber drivers seek to maintain their online reputation by asking passengers to leave a (positive) review (Kuhn & Maleki, 2017; Rosenblat, 2018). The effect of such initiatives may, however, be mixed, as some consumers might find this disturbing and therefore do not leave an online review or even post a negative review. In contrast, others see it as a call to leave a review, mainly when they are satisfied with the gig worker's performance.

Third, online platforms such as Airbnb, Werkspot, and HiHiGuide show the volume (i.e., the number) of reviews a gig worker has received in the past. Research has shown that online review volume impacts consumer behaviour. For instance, Kostyra, Reiner, Natter, and Klapper (2016) show that products are more likely to be bought when their average rating improves. However, this effect weakens as review volume for a selected product increases (Kostyra et al., 2016). In line with this, it can be expected that the amount of reviews of a gig worker is negatively related to the number of reviews s/he receives in the future. Here, consumers might perceive the marginal effect (in terms of changing a gig worker's online reputation) of leaving a review for a gig worker that has previously gained a substantial amount of reviews as low. In such cases, a consumer might be less likely to leave an online review.

Finally, the given average rating on a scale from 1 to 5 of a gig worker—which represents average customer satisfaction and reflects a workers' online reputation—likely impacts online reviewing by consumers. Consumers may be less likely to leave a review when their experience with a gig worker does not match the average rating of a gig worker, as this creates cognitive dissonance. Cognitive dissonance refers to the mental discomfort experienced by a person whose beliefs clash with the new evidence presented to that person (Festinger, 1957). In the gig economy, consumers' views about a gig worker are shaped by online reviews, as consumers strongly rely on available reviews to make purchase-related decisions (Ert, Fleischer, & Magen, 2016; Ter Huurne, Ronteltap, Corten, & Buskens, 2017). If these beliefs do not match the actual performance of a gig worker, then a consumer might be less likely to leave a review as this makes cognitive dissonance more salient. Previous customer reviews (indirectly) establish performance expectations—creating a situation whereby reputational value precedes the performance of the service/task.

Consumer-Level Antecedents

A variety of consumer attributes may explain the likelihood of online appraisal by consumers on online labour platforms. A vital characteristic may be a consumer's exchange orientation. According to Buunk and Van Yperen (1991:802), exchange orientation refers to 'the personality disposition of individuals who are strongly oriented to direct reciprocation, who expect immediate and comparable rewards when they have provided rewards to others, and who feel uncomfortable when they receive favours they cannot immediately reciprocate.' In comparison, in e-commerce platforms where products are transacted, the role of exchange orientation is likely to be important in the gig economy context, because platform-mediated labour involves humans offering a service on a recurrent basis (e.g., meal deliverers servicing restaurants or housekeeping professionals cleaning a property weekly). This creates social exchange processes, where consumers and gig workers may reciprocate each other's efforts. As an example, Wood et al. (2019) show that consumers, when granting orders, return gig workers' past performance by favouring high-performing workers. These reciprocal acts may also drive online reviewing, where consumers reciprocate high-level gig worker performance by leaving a (positive) online review. Such mutual actions are more likely to occur among consumers who score high on exchange orientation. Moreover, a consumer with a high exchange orientation may more likely engage in online reviewing to reciprocate the online reviews of his/her peers which the focal consumer relied on to make purchase-related decisions (Ert et al., 2016; Ter Huurne et al., 2017).

The motives of consumers to rely on online (labour) platforms likely play a role in explaining online reviewing habits. Research shows that these motives relate to issues such as convenience, utility, transaction costs, and meeting new people (Hamari, Sjöklint, & Ukkonen, 2016; Möhlmann, 2015). Depending on these motives, consumers may have different expectations of gig workers and, thus, differ in the degree to which they experience high-quality service provision. These service quality perceptions, in turn, explain whether consumers leave a review (Dellarocas & Wood, 2008; Meijerink & Schoenmakers, 2020). In line with this, research has shown that consumers' abilities relate positively to their perceptions of the service quality of technology-mediated services (Van Beuningen, De Ruyter, Wetzels, & Streukens, 2009). This implies that consumers with high-level abilities and long-term experience in making use of an online platform and/or gig work experience higher levels of service quality and, therefore, are more likely to leave (positive) reviews. In support of this, Horton and Golden (2015) show that, over time, online reviews on online labour platforms—such as oDesk and Elance—tend to become more positive.

Finally, online reviewing habits may be dependent on consumers' attributions about why online labour platforms request online reviews. Online platforms rely on online reviews to create trust, deactivate gig workers, improve service provision, and/or match workers with consumers based on their online reputation (Kuhn & Maleki, 2017; Lee et al., 2015; Rosenblat, 2018). In line with the work of Nishii, Lepak, and Schneider (2008), I propose that consumers—as important HRM players in the gig economy—may develop at least two types of attributions why platforms rely on online reviews: commitment-focused attributions (e.g., to create trust, to improve service provision) and control-focused attributions (to exploit gig workers, to capture disproportionate value from consumers/workers). Provided that individuals respond more positively to commitment-focused attributions than control-focused attributions (Nishii et al., 2008; Van De Voorde & Beijer, 2015), I expect that consumers are more likely to leave online reviews when they develop commitment-focused attributions.

Platform-Level Antecedents

Various design features and attributes of the online platform or firm play a role in explaining online reviewing habits by consumers. First, the privacy and anonymity of online reviews influence the motivation of consumers to leave (negative) online reviews (Bridges & Vásquez, 2018; Horton & Golden, 2015). Platforms such as Uber and Deliveroo, which algorithmically dispatch orders, keep the reviews of individual consumers private by aggregating consumer reviews to an average rating per gig worker. Other platforms that offer consumers the freedom to select a gig worker—like Airbnb, Werkspot, and HiHiGuide—make (written) reviews publicly available. The field experiment by Horton and Golden (2015) shows that consumers who had negative experiences with gig workers are more likely to leave (negative) reviews when their reviews are kept private by the platform firm as compared to when reviews are shared in public.

Second, platform firms offer rewards to induce consumers to leave an online review. These rewards can be both monetary (e.g., coupons, discounts) as well non-monetary (e.g., assign a 'superior' status to consumers who frequently leave reviews) (Fradkin et al., 2018; Teubner & Glaser, 2018). Research shows that such rewards influence the likelihood of consumers leaving online reviews. For instance, Fradkin et al. (2018) conducted a field experiment which showed that consumers of Airbnb who were offered a $25 Airbnb coupon in exchange for a review left online reviews more often than those who were not offered this coupon. Moreover, offering a coupon increases the likelihood that dissatisfied consumers leave a (negative) review, which implies that online reputation inflation can be partially offset by offering monetary rewards in exchange for a review (Fradkin et al., 2018).

Finally, platform firms differ in whether they let consumers and workers mutually evaluate one another. For instance, whereas Uber drivers get to evaluate passengers, in many meal delivery platforms, such as Deliveroo and Uber Eats, gig workers are evaluated by consumers, but not vice versa. Mutual performance appraisal may lead gig workers to strategically induce reciprocal responses from consumers. This may happen, for instance, when a gig worker leaves a positive review of a consumer hoping that the consumer will reciprocate the act by also leaving a (positive) review (Fradkin et al., 2018; Rosenblat & Stark, 2016).

Where to Next for Academics?

Viewing online appraisal by consumers as a multilevel phenomenon, and clustering its antecedents on different levels of analysis opens the road for new research initiatives on performance appraisal on online labour platforms. Here, the multilevel theory is beneficial, as it offers multilevel principles that can be applied to derive questions for future research. These principles revolve around the what, how, when, where, and why of multilevel relationships (Klein & Kozlowski, 2000; Renkema et al., 2017). Below, I discuss these principles and how these can be translated into novel research questions/avenues on online reviewing by consumers of online labour platforms.

The 'What' of Online Appraisal by Consumers

The 'what' principle concerns the level at which the phenomenon of interest is manifested (Klein & Kozlowski, 2000; Renkema et al., 2017). In the case of online appraisal, consumer reviews manifest at the level of transaction/worker, consumer, and online platform (see Figure 6.1). Klein and Kozlowski (2000) recommend researchers to start their multilevel analysis by defining and justifying the level at which the variable of interest resides. Accordingly, future research needs to uncover at which level the majority of variance in online reviews lies. In my view, the majority of variation in online reviews by consumers resides on the worker/transaction level, since consumers of online labour platforms are matchmade with different workers.

Moreover, the primary purpose of online labour platforms is to spark repeated transactions (Friedman, 2014; Kuhn & Maleki, 2017; Stanford, 2017). It is the transactions and the workers offering freelance services that are evaluated. This implies that the majority of variance in online reviewing resides on the transaction/worker level. In line with this, future academic studies must seek to answer research questions such as: how is the variance in online reviews by customers distributed across the transaction, consumer, and platform level? To what extent does the majority in this variance reside on the transaction level? Is the percentage of variance in online reviews the lowest on the platform-level? Are different online platforms similar in the percentage of transactions that ultimately get evaluated?

The 'How' of Online Appraisal by Consumers

The 'how' principle describes how two or more levels are linked, that is, through top-down and/or bottom-up processes (Klein & Kozlowski,

2000; Renkema et al., 2017). Top-down processes describe the influence of higher-level contextual factors on lower-level phenomena. In the case of online reviewing, top-down effects occur when the platform and/or consumer attributes influence whether a consumer evaluates a gig worker or a transaction. Bottom-up effects manifest through so-called emergence processes through which lower-level phenomena aggregate to higher-levels of analysis. Bottom-up emergence occurs through either composition (i.e., individual-level phenomena remaining the same as these aggregate to a higher level) or compilation (i.e., individual-level phenomena sharing a common domain but remaining distinctively different across levels) (Ployhart & Moliterno, 2011; Renkema et al., 2017). In line with this, future research could examine whether online reviews emerge from the transaction level to the consumer level and onwards to the platform level through a process of composition or compilation. As such, relevant questions are whether an individual consumer leaves both positive and negative reviews (i.e., compilation) versus only negative or positive reviews (i.e., composition), as well as whether online reviews on the platform level tend to become homogenous and positive (i.e., composition) versus being a mix between negative and positive reviews (i.e., compilation).

In explaining how online reviews emerge to a higher level of analysis, research may draw on the notion of emergence *structure,* which describes the higher-level contextual factors that shape the process of emergence (Klein & Kozlowski, 2000). In the case of an online review, emergence structure reflects the attributes of the online platform or firm. In line with this, future research could examine whether online reviews emerge to the platform level through compilation or composition and on which platform-level characteristics this is dependent. For instance, Horton and Golden (2015) show that online reviews on the platform level tend to become more positive and homogenous over time (i.e., composition-based emergence). They attribute this to the fact that online reviewing is not anonymous, which demotivates dissatisfied consumers to leave a review. Building on their results, researchers could ask the question of whether online reviews emerge through a process of compilation (i.e., being more heterogeneous on the platform level) when online labour platforms decide to solicit anonymous reviews.

The 'Where' of Online Appraisal by Consumers

The 'where' principle describes where multilevel relationships originate and culminate (Klein & Kozlowski, 2000; Renkema et al., 2017). This principle can be studied using the concept of *bond strength,* which refers to the extent to which variables at one level of analysis affect the outcomes on another level. The notion of bond strength predicts that relationships between levels of analysis are stronger when these levels are more proximate (Klein & Kozlowski, 2000). Bond strength can, therefore, be considered to predict how strongly variables on different levels of analysis are related. In line with the notion of bond strength, platform-level attributes (e.g., incentives for inducing reviews or technical design of the review application) are more strongly linked with online reviewing on the consumer level (i.e., review propensity) than with reviewing on the transaction level—as the latter level is more distal to the platform level. On this basis, researchers could ask the following research questions: are customer attributes more strongly linked to online reviewing habits on the worker/transaction level in comparison to platform-level attributes? Is the link between platform-level attributes and online reviewing on the transaction level weaker than the link between customer-level attributes and online reviewing habits on the transaction level? To what extent do attributes on the platform and consumer level explain variance in online customer reviews on the transaction level?

The 'When' of Online Appraisal by Consumers

The 'when' principle centres on the role of time in multilevel re-lationships. According to Klein and Kozlowski (2000), time can be seen as a *boundary condition* that specifies the direction of multilevel relationships. For instance, changes in the technical design of review systems (i.e., a platform-level phenomenon) may have a rapid top-down effect on the online appraisal of transactions. The time needed for the changes in transaction-level reviews to emerge and alter the review density on the platform level may take place later in time. For instance, the results of Horton and Golden (2015) show that at least four years passed before the customer reviews on oDesk and Elance platforms became more or less consistent across transactions (i.e., for composition emergence to occur). In line with this, future studies could theorise and empirically explore whether top-down effects manifest predominantly right after the platform or a change in its review system 'went live,' with bottom-up effects occurring in later stages. Moreover, researchers need to answer questions such as: how much time (e.g., in weeks, months, or years does it take for changes in the technical design of review systems (i.e., or a platform-level phenomenon to result in changes in the online appraisal of transactions? How much time does it take before changes in transaction-level reviews emerge to changes in review propensity or review density?

Furthermore, researchers could examine 'time-scale variation across levels,' which reflects the time needed before an event occurs on other levels of analysis (Klein & Kozlowski, 2000). Given the sheer number of transactions taking place on online labour platforms, it will likely take time before changes in reviews on the transaction level emerge to, and, thus, cause changes in the aggregate reviews on the platform level (i.e., review density). In line with this, future research could examine how long it takes before changes in online reviews on lower levels of analysis results in changes in reviews on higher levels of analysis and whether this is contingent on emerge structure (i.e., or the attributes of the online platform (firm)).

The 'Why' of Online Appraisal by Consumers

The 'why' principle stresses the need for researchers to provide theoretical explanations for the multilevel relationship under study (Klein & Kozlowski, 2000; Renkema et al., 2017). Since most online review systems are easy to use, consumer abilities likely explain only a small portion of the variance in customer online reviewing habits. Instead, examining consumers' willingness to leave only reviews is more promising, making motivation-based theories suitable for explaining the multilevel effects in online reviewing habits of consumers of online labour platforms.

Here, the self-determination theory may explain how worker, consumer, and platform attributes relate to online reviewing habits. The self-determination theory proposes four types of extrinsic motivation—which differ in their relative autonomy and, thus, the degree to which they motivate action (Deci & Ryan, 2000). The least autonomous type of extrinsic motivation is *external regulation,* which drives behaviour through external demand and possible reward. In online labour platform contexts, external regulation thus explains how rewarding consumers (e.g., through coupons) influences online reviewing *Introjected regulation* is slightly more autonomous and reflects the idea that individuals are motivated to showcase their ability to maintain self-worth. Online labour platforms that make online reviews publicly available provide consumers with the opportunity to showcase their capability to acquire online services, appraise gig worker performance, or sanction poor performance. This implies that platform-level attributes, such as the technical design of an online reviewing system, relate to online reviewing through the mediating role of introjected regulation. The remaining motivational states of *regulated identification* (e.g., valuing a goal or regulation) and *integrated regulation* (internalised norms and values) are autonomous and come from within the individual (Deci & Ryan, 2000). These are, therefore, more likely to explain how consumer-level attributes (e.g., personality traits, exchange orientation) relate to online reviewing habits. In line with this, future academic studies may address essential research questions like to which extent do the four types of extrinsic motivation differ in their validity to explain how customer and platform attributes relate to online review outcomes on lower levels of analysis? Is customer motivation a better predictor of online customer reviews than customer ability?

While the self-determination theory can explain top-down processes in multilevel online reviewing, the attraction-selection-attrition (ASA) theory may explain bottom-up effects (Schneider, 1987). The ASA theory predicts that individuals become more homogenous in their perceptions and behaviours as individuals with similar backgrounds, expectations, orientations, and characteristics feel attracted to an organisation and are selected by organisation members who are similar to them. In contrast, those who are different from the group members will leave. The same case may occur with the consumers and workers of online labour platforms: some consumers feel more attracted to a platform and select workers who are similar to them. Consumers and workers who do not fit this may leave the platform. Over time, this creates a homogenous set of workers and consumers who understand one another's interests and needs, which results in (perceived) high-quality service provision. Ultimately, this may drive compositional emergence where only positive reviews emerge on the platform level. In support of this claim, Teubner and Glaser (2018) show that, over time, review scores on Airbnb become more homogenous (and positive), and this is attributed to the attrition of poor service providers and those with limited reviews being selected out of the market. Accordingly, future research would benefit from answering research questions such as: to which extent do online customer reviews on the platform level become more homogenous over time? Which platform attributes best explain why these homogenisation processes occur?

Where to Next for Practitioners?

The multilevel framework of online appraisal by consumers has implications for gig workers, consumers, and platform firms. First, for gig workers, it helps to show that their (perceived) value and whether they are classified as talented are dependent on a range of variables. The multilevel framework can assist them in bringing back the plethora of variables into three meaningful categories—these are worker, consumer, and platform attributions. Based on this, gig workers can develop proactive strategies that are instrumental in soliciting (positive) customer reviews. Besides seeking to offer high-quality services, such approaches may include asking for a review from customers whose attributes reduce the likelihood of leaving reviews (e.g., consumers with a low exchange orientation) or explaining why the platform firm solicits online reviews for shaping consumers' attributions. Moreover, the multilevel framework may offer (potential) gig workers a tool to decide which online platform/s they want to join. In doing so, they could consider the technical features of the online platform firms' review system that benefit gig workers (e.g., non-anonymous reviews by customers).

Second, the multilevel framework helps make consumers aware of their role in talent identification and evaluation in the gig economy. More specifically, it spells out which consumer attributions encourage or discourage consumers from leaving reviews on an online labour platform. It might be helpful for consumers to be aware of these attributions to avoid, for example, reputation inflation. For instance, a consumer who scores low on exchange orientation may be less likely to leave a review after s/he experienced poor service quality levels. Being aware of this might help to ensure that gig workers are evaluated appropriately.

Moreover, the role of past reviews and a gig worker's online reputation are likely to affect the likelihood that a consumer reviews a transaction. It is suitable for consumers to realise that their reviews can have a substantial marginal effect—in particular, when their experience differs from those reported by other consumers. Ultimately, consumers must leave reviews that reflect the service quality provided by a gig worker to ensure that online reviews reliably reflect the value of a gig worker.

Finally, the multilevel framework has implications for online platform firms and those who design online customer review technologies. Specifically, some of the features designed into online review systems may refrain customers from leaving online reviews. For instance, by making reviews non-anonymous, consumers may feel less likely to share their negative experiences. At the same time, having non-anonymous reviews may help to create the trust needed by future customers to hire a gig worker (Pavlou & Gefen, 2004). As such, online labour platforms likely have to make a trade-off between making reviews public to stimulate ongoing exchanges on the platform versus making reviews anonymous to ensure that customers feel comfortable to leave negative reviews.

Furthermore, online platforms have to consider the number of reviews that add to the online reputation of a gig worker for motivating consumers to leave an online review. For instance, if online reputations are based on the latest 500 reviews received by a worker, then consumers might feel that the marginal effect of their review is low. As such, online platforms may want to limit the number of reviews included in an average review score, as much as possible, but without making a gig worker's online reputation heavily dependent on those few reviews. Finally, online platforms may want to be clear in their communication with consumers on the purpose of online reviews. Here, a consumer might be less likely to leave online reviews when they believe that online reviews exploit gig workers or sanction workers without human intervention. Instead, online platforms may want to stress that online reviews are used to improve customer experiences and to improve gig worker performance—and, most importantly, live up to these promises—to induce online customer reviews.

Conclusion

By drawing on multilevel theory, this chapter presents a conceptual, multilevel framework on the drivers that explain why consumers engage in online appraisal in the gig economy. Online appraisal is proposed to manifest on three levels: the worker/transaction level, the consumer level, and the platform level. In line with this, the drivers of online appraisal by consumers in the gig economy can be grouped into three clusters or levels of analysis: platform attributes (e.g., rewards and technical design of the online review system), consumer attributes (e.g., personality traits and orientations), and interaction level (e.g., performance/behaviour and online reputation of a worker). Although online reviewing habits on online platforms are studied extensively, this chapter is the first to cluster relevant antecedents into meaningful clusters. Moreover, by adopting a multilevel theoretical perspective, this chapter opens the road for answering important and novel research questions on the what, how, where, when, and why of multilevel effects of the platform, consumer, and worker attributes on online reviewing habits.

References

Aloisi, A. (2016). Commoditized workers: Case study research on labor law issues arising from a set of on-demand/gig economy platforms. *Comparative Labor Law & Policy Journal, 37*(3), 653–690.

Bridges, J., & Vásquez, C. (2018). If nearly all Airbnb reviews are positive, does that make them meaningless? *Current Issues in Tourism, 21*(18), 2057–2075.

Buunk, B. P., & Van Yperen, N. W. (1991). Referential comparisons, relational comparisons, and exchange orientation: Their relation to marital satisfaction. *Personality and Social Psychology Bulletin, 17*(6), 709–717.

Cassady, E. A., Fisher, S. L., & Olsen, S. (2018). Using eHRM to manage workers in the platform economy. *The Brave New World of eHRM 2.0*, 217.

Collings, D. G., & Mellahi, K. (2009). Strategic talent management: A review and research agenda. *Human Resource Management Review, 19*(4), 304–313.

Daskalova, V. (2018). Regulating the new self-employed in the uber economy: What role for EU competition law. *German Law Journal, 19*, 461.

Deci, E. L., & Ryan, R. M. (2000). The "what" and "why" of goal pursuits: Human needs and the self-determination of behavior. *Psychological Inquiry, 11*(4), 227–268.

Dellarocas, C., & Narayan, R. (2006). A statistical measure of a population's propensity to engage in post-purchase online word-of-mouth. *Statistical Science, 21*(2), 277–285.

Dellarocas, C., & Wood, C. A. (2008). The sound of silence in online feedback: Estimating trading risks in the presence of reporting bias. *Management Science, 54*(3), 460–476.

Duggan, J., Sherman, U., Carbery, R., & McDonnell, A. (2019). Algorithmic management & app-work in the gig economy: A research agenda for employment relations & HRM. *Human Resource Management Journal, 30*(1), 114–132. doi: 10.1111/1748-8583.12258.

Ellmer, M., & Reichel, A. (2018). *Crowdwork from an HRM perspective–integrating organizational performance and employee welfare.* University of Salzburg: Working Paper, 1.

Ert, E., Fleischer, A., & Magen, N. (2016). Trust and reputation in the sharing economy: The role of personal photos in Airbnb. *Tourism Management, 55*, 62–73.

Festinger, L. (1957). *A theory of cognitive dissonance.* Evanston: Rew, Peterson.

Fradkin, A., Grewal, E., & Holtz, D. (2018). *The determinants of online review informativeness: Evidence from field experiments on Airbnb.* Available at SSRN: https://ssrn.com/abstract=2939064 or http://dx.doi.org/10.2139/ssrn.2939064.

Friedman, G. (2014). Workers without employers: Shadow corporations and the rise of the gig economy. *Review of Keynesian Economics, 2*(2), 171–188.

Gawer, A., & Cusumano, M. A. (2002). *Platform leadership: How Intel, Microsoft, and Cisco drive industry innovation.* Boston, MA: Harvard Business School Press.

Hamari, J., Sjöklint, M., & Ukkonen, A. (2016). The sharing economy: Why people participate in collaborative consumption. *Journal of the Association for Information Science and Technology, 67*(9), 2047–2059.

Horton, J., & Golden, J. (2015). *Reputation inflation: Evidence from an online labor market.* Working paper, NYU.

Jacobides, M. G., Cennamo, C., & Gawer, A. (2018). Towards a theory of ecosystems. *Strategic Management Journal, 39*(8), 2255–2276. doi:10.1002/smj.2904.

Klein, K. J., & Kozlowski, S. W. (2000). *Multilevel theory, research, and methods in organizations: Foundations, extensions, and new directions.* San Francisco, CA: Jossey-Bass.

Kostyra, D. S., Reiner, J., Natter, M., & Klapper, D. (2016). Decomposing the effects of online customer reviews on brand, price, and product attributes. *International Journal of Research in Marketing, 33*(1), 11–26.

Kuhn, K. M., & Maleki, A. (2017). Micro-entrepreneurs, dependent contractors, and instaserfs: Understanding online labor platform workforces. *The Academy of Management Perspectives, 31*(3), 183–200.

Lee, E., & Lee, B. (2012). Herding behavior in online P2P lending: An empirical investigation. *Electronic Commerce Research and Applications, 11*(5), 495–503.

Lee, M. K., Kusbit, D., Metsky, E., & Dabbish, L. (2015). *Working with machines: The impact of algorithmic and data-driven management on human workers.* Paper presented at the Proceedings of the *33rd Annual ACM Conference on Human Factors in Computing Systems*, New York.

Lehdonvirta, V., Kässi, O., Hjorth, I., Barnard, H., & Graham, M. (2018). The global platform economy: A new offshoring institution enabling emerging-economy microproviders, *Journal of Management, 45*(2), 567–599. doi:10.1177/0149206318786781.

Meijerink, J. G., & Keegan, A. (2019). Conceptualizing human resource management in the gig economy: Toward a platform ecosystem perspective. *Journal of Managerial Psychology, 34*(4), 214–232.

Meijerink, J. G., Keegan, A., & Bondarouk, T. (2019). *Exploring 'human resource management without employment' in the gig economy: How online labor platforms manage institutional complexity.* Paper presented at the *6th International Workshop on the Sharing Economy Utrecht*, The Netherlands, June 28–29, 2019.

Meijerink, J. G., & Schoenmakers, E. (2020). Why are online reviews in the sharing economy skewed toward positive ratings? Linking customer perceptions of service quality to leaving a review of an Airbnb stay. *Journal of Tourism Futures.* In press.

Meyers, M. C., & van Woerkom, M. (2014). The influence of underlying philosophies on talent management: Theory, implications for practice, and research agenda. *Journal of World Business, 49*(2), 192–203.

Möhlmann, M. (2015). Collaborative consumption: Determinants of satisfaction and the likelihood of using a sharing economy option again. *Journal of Consumer Behaviour, 14*(3), 193–207.

Mowen, J. C., Park, S., & Zablah, A. (2007). Toward a theory of motivation and personality with application to word-of-mouth communications. *Journal of Business Research, 60*(6), 590–596.

Newlands, G., Lutz, C., & Fieseler, C. (2018). *European perspectives on power in the sharing economy*. Retrieved from http://dx.doi.org/10.2139/ssrn. 3046473.

Nishii, L. H., Lepak, D. P., & Schneider, B. (2008). Employee attributions of the "why" of HR practices: Their effects on employee attitudes and behaviors, and customer satisfaction. *Personnel Psychology, 61*(3), 503–545.

Parker, G. G., & Van Alstyne, M. W. (2005). Two-sided network effects: A theory of information product design. *Management Science, 51*(10), 1494–1504.

Pavlou, P. A., & Gefen, D. (2004). Building effective online marketplaces with institution-based trust. *Information Systems Research, 15*(1), 37–59.

Ployhart, R. E., & Moliterno, T. P. (2011). Emergence of the human capital resource: A multilevel model. *Academy of Management Review, 36*(1), 127–150.

Renkema, M., Meijerink, J., & Bondarouk, T. (2017). Advancing multilevel thinking in human resource management research: Applications and guidelines. *Human Resource Management Review, 27*(3), 397–415. doi:10. 1016/j.hrmr.2017.03.001.

Rosenblat, A. (2018). *Uberland: How algorithms are rewriting the rules of work*. Oakland: University of California Press.

Rosenblat, A., Levy, K. E., Barocas, S., & Hwang, T. (2017). Discriminating tastes: Uber's customer ratings as vehicles for workplace discrimination. *Policy & Internet, 9*(3), 256–279.

Rosenblat, A., & Stark, L. (2016). Algorithmic labor and information asymmetries: A case study of Uber's drivers. *International Journal of Communication, 10*(27), 3758–3784.

Schneider, B. (1987). The people make the place. *Personnel Psychology, 40*(3), 437–453.

Stanford, J. (2017). The resurgence of gig work: Historical and theoretical perspectives. *The Economic and Labour Relations Review, 28*(3), 382–401.

Ter Huurne, M., Ronteltap, A., Corten, R., & Buskens, V. (2017). Antecedents of trust in the sharing economy: A systematic review. *Journal of Consumer Behaviour, 16*(6), 485–498.

Teubner, T., & Glaser, F. (2018). *Up or out–the dynamics of star rating scores on Airbnb*. Paper presented at the *Twenty-Sixth European Conference on Information Systems*, Portsmouth, UK.

Van Beuningen, J., De Ruyter, K., Wetzels, M., & Streukens, S. (2009). Customer self-efficacy in technology-based self-service: Assessing between- and within-person differences. *Journal of Service Research, 11*(4), 407–428.

Van De Voorde, K., & Beijer, S. (2015). The role of employee HR attributions in the relationship between high-performance work systems and employee outcomes. *Human Resource Management Journal, 25*(1), 62–78.

Wood, A. J., Graham, M., Lehdonvirta, V., & Hjorth, I. (2019). Good gig, bad gig: Autonomy and algorithmic control in the global gig economy. *Work, Employment and Society, 33*(1), 56–75.

Zervas, G., Proserpio, D., & Byers, J. (2015). A first look at online reputation on Airbnb, where every stay is above average. *SSRN Electronic Journal.* doi: 10.2139/ssrn.2554500.

7 Artificial Intelligence and Talent Management

Andy Charlwood

> **If I Could Say One Thing:**
> *Ultimately, the use of AI in talent management is likely to reflect the values of the businesses introducing it and the societies they operate in. Therefore, we all have a responsibility to speak up for the values that matter to us.*
>
> —Andy Charlwood

Introduction

It is claimed that artificial intelligence (AI) is on the cusp of transforming talent management and the broader HR function (Guenole & Feinzig, 2019). The last decade has seen profound advancements in the deployment of artificial intelligence technology. As a result, there is a thriving ecosystem of innovators, computer scientists, technologists, entrepreneurs, and venture capitalists developing new products and services that deploy (or claim to deploy) AI technology for people management tasks and activities. A recent industry study found more than 300 HR technology start-ups that were developing AI tools and products for people management—with around 60 of these companies 'gaining traction' in terms of customers and venture capital funding (Bailie & Butler, 2018). In this context, this chapter aims to address three key questions. First, what is artificial intelligence (AI)? Second, how might AI be used in talent management, and what are its potential benefits? Third, what are the likely barriers to the adoption of AI in talent management that may result in some organisations lagging? Answering these questions will advance the argument that, despite the promise of AI for talent management, there are several barriers—both technological and ethical/legal—that may prevent organisations from adopting it.

What is AI?

There is no one universal definition of AI. Still, a common thread linking many existing definitions is that AI is the science and engineering of machines that can do tasks that have hitherto required human intelligence—for example, visual perception and recognising speech (Bailie & Butler, 2018:9–10). Early representations of AI in science fiction suggest a technology that is directly akin, yet superior, to human intelligence. The reality of AI as it currently exists is very different from science fiction. It is not artificial general intelligence of the type that could pass the 'Turing test' of being sufficiently human-like, that a human could converse with it without realising that they were not talking to a fellow human. Most technologies classed as AI typically rely on algorithms known as artificial neural networks. Artificial neural networks use a process known as backward propagation to learn how to classify sounds, images, text, or other data by identifying characteristics within a training dataset (Somers, 2017). This classification allows for prediction. If an AI 'hears' the sounds that make up the question 'what is the weather like in Leeds today?' then it predicts that those sounds are a question about the weather and can then follow a decision rule to provide an answer.

Similarly, if an AI has been trained on millions of images of human cells—some of which are cancerous and some of which are not—then it can then predict whether new images contain cancerous cells. If an AI can be provided with enough of the right sort of data to predict something accurately, then the cost of each subsequent prediction falls to near zero. Therefore, AI heralds an age of cheap prediction (Agrawal, Gans, & Goldfarb, 2018, 2019).

This is considered to be artificial intelligence, because—in contrast to supervised machine learning where the programmer specifies pre-defined parameters for the algorithmic analysis—artificial neural networks and analogous approaches develop predictions without human intervention or instruction from observing data. For example, the first computers to be able to beat people at chess were first programmed on how to play the game. In contrast, AI-powered machines like Google's DeepMind can learn how to play chess and other much more complex games without humans programming them with the game rules (Cookson, 2018).

For strictly defined AIs that are based around unsupervised machine learning algorithms, the critical issue is whether the AI can be provided with enough data to make an accurate prediction. Although an AI first drove a car autonomously in 2005 (Bailie & Butler, 2018:12), at the time of writing, AI has not yet learned how to drive a car within acceptable safety parameters for AI-driven cars to be allowed on public roads. This is because of the sheer volume of different factors that could be experienced when driving, and the task requires more data than those developing driving AIs have been able to collect and process. However, AIs have been used successfully to provide safety aids to human drivers—for example, by predicting and warning when a car or a pedestrian is likely to be in a driver's blind spot. AIs are also driving vehicles autonomously in more predictable and controlled environments—for example, in warehouses. The point here is that, while AIs are often very good at prediction, they are best used in conjunction with human expertise. AIs can predict, but human input is often needed to decide based on the prediction. The more complex the prediction task, the greater the need for human input in decision-making (Agrawal et al., 2018, 2019).

While the basic concepts behind artificial neural networks were discovered in the 1970s and developed in the 1980s, significant advancements in the deployment of AIs have only begun to happen within the last ten years—as a result of an explosion in the volume of data available to train AIs on and the steady advancements in computer processing and data storage technologies (Agrawal et al., 2018; Somers, 2017:8). This means that the full potential and impact of AI has yet to be felt or perhaps even imagined; AI is, therefore, best conceived of as new general-purpose technology. Economic and business history tells us that the full effects of new general-purpose technologies take time to be felt, advance unevenly, and develop in ways that are often unpredictable at the outset because they depend on complementary innovations in skills and technology (Brynjolfsson, Rock, & Syverson, 2017). Although AI can be considered conceptually distinct from supervised machine learning algorithms, in practice, AI may be used as a catch-all term to encompass any machine learning algorithm. This can make the discussion of AI in talent management confusing at times, because some of the software as service products for talent management that are in development are described as AI even when the product appears to be based around supervised machine learning. Given these distinctions and points for confusion, the conceptual focus of this chapter is on AI as unsupervised machine learning, but some of the discussion of current applications may reference examples of supervised machine learning. With these opportunities and difficulties in mind, we now turn to the question of how AI might be deployed in talent management.

How Might AI Be Used in Talent Management?

A useful starting point for thinking about how AI might be used in talent management is Strohmeier and Piazza's (2015) conceptual exploration of how AI might be applied to human resource management. They suggest six specific uses: predicting which employees will quit, candidate search, processing CVs and application forms, staff rostering, sentiment analysis, and employee self-service through chatbots. The first three of these are particularly germane to the issue of talent management, while employee self-service through chatbots could have a role in talent development. There is also evidence that talent acquisition and selection are the areas that HR professionals looking to implement AI in their organisations are most focused on (Bailie & Butler, 2018:17).

Talent Acquisition and Selection

Talent acquisition and selection are the areas that AI appears to be making the most immediate impact in. This is perhaps unsurprising, given that the vast majority of technology spent on people management activities is within the domains of recruitment, selection, and talent acquisition. Selection is a prediction task, so it is theoretically well-suited to AI. Selection decisions made by humans are often done with a range of biases and implicit beliefs (Highhouse, 2008), suggesting there is scope for AI to help to improve human decision-making if AI can find ways of reducing bias (Cowgill, 2018). Third, selection is a time-consuming and, therefore, expensive business. The time and cost of selection necessarily limit the talent pools from which organisations select from, and this perhaps means that they consider a narrower range of candidates than is optimal. The low cost of AI-based prediction could potentially dramatically lower the cost of selection while allowing organisations to select from a broader range of candidates.

At the time of writing, the most prominent example of this use of AI in talent acquisition and selection is done by Unilever who, since 2017, has been using AI-based methods to select candidates for its global graduate management training program. The first stage of the AI-based process is for candidates to play a series of short games designed to test cognitive ability. Candidates who are successful at this stage then participate in video interviews. The AI that analyses the video interviews has already been trained on video interviews with existing high-performing employees who are part of previous cohorts of the graduate training program. The AI ranks candidates based on interview performance to create a shortlist for in-person assessment centres. Traditional interpersonal methods then complete the final stage of the selection process. Unilever claims that this application of AI has been a dramatic success. The selection process has become faster, and those recruited were more ethnically and educationally diverse than previous cohorts. Candidates were also satisfied with the process because they appreciated the speed with which it was completed and the fact that they were able to get quick and meaningful feedback on their applications as a result of the automation of the process (Simms, 2019).

Beyond this single example from practice, there is also scientific evidence that using machine learning as support to human decision-making in candidate selection can result in both greater efficiencies and the selection of a more diverse group of candidates than traditional interpersonal methods alone. A key concern with using AI for selection is that AIs will learn from training data that reflects existing biases in human decision-making, so discriminatory practices are perpetuated (more on this will be elaborated on in the next section). However, decision-making is not just subject to bias, but it is also affected by random noise (e.g. What is the weather like, is it a sunny day? Did the decision-maker have an argument with their spouse or children before they came to work? Do they have a headache?). AI can potentially use random noise to detect and remove bias, an approach taken by Cowgill (2018). Empirically, when machine-derived recommendations for which applicants would be interviewed were compared to human-derived recommendations, machine-based recommendations were more diverse, perhaps because the algorithm gave greater weight to work experience and less to educational credentials. In contrast, human decision-makers privileged particular types of educational credentials. Machine-recommended candidates were then more likely to receive a job offer from the later interpersonal stages of the selection process.

While the theory in Cowgill's paper could potentially apply to selection AI, it is perhaps noteworthy to says that the empirical test of the theory came from a human-designed experiment on a human-designed algorithm rather than unsupervised machine learning. As Cowgill points out, human expertise is encoded in the development of the algorithm he tested; the machine can learn because an expert psychologist decided to ask job candidates a question that was likely to yield information that the machine can use as the basis of a prediction.

Similarly, with the Unilever case, the basis of AI predictions were tests developed using existing employees that Unilever believed to be its strongest performers. The AI is encoding the expert judgment about what makes for a good employee of Unilever's recruiters rather than engaging in totally unsupervised learning. If AI is to be applied to talent management, then all of this points to the importance of human decisions made about the training data used to teach AIs if the AI is to reach fair and efficient predictions.

Talent Development

Traditionally, organisations' internal talent management programs have been rather elitist. A relatively small group of employees are identified as 'high potential talent' and then are hothoused through talent development programs that are designed to give them the breadth of skills, experience, support, and networks to advance to senior leadership positions in the future. The elitist nature of these programs reflects the costs of delivering them. It also reduces the cognitive load on managers and their HR advisors tasked with appointing the leaders of the future by providing a clearly defined talent pool from which to select; large talent pools risk overwhelming decision-makers. AI has the potential to democratise talent management programmes in three key ways. First, AI could analyse the skills and experience needed to rise to senior leadership positions—predicting the skills and knowledge that talent management programmes need to deliver. Second, it could disseminate this information widely and affordably through chatbots that provide guidance and mentoring (e.g. predicting the skills, knowledge, and experience that individual employees need to develop), allowing more employees to participate in talent management programs. Such chatbots are not able to pass the Turing test. i.e., those who interact with them will not mistake the bot for a person. Instead, they provide a relatively user-friendly and, therefore, efficient way of interacting with a wider body of complex knowledge. Third, it could help decision-makers sift through the new and larger talent pool to identify who should be considered for senior leadership positions by predicting who are likely to succeed in these roles.

A couple of HR technology start-ups are offering products in this space. Qweek is an AI-powered product that analyses users' spoken and written communications and provides coaching on how to improve communication skills, while Sidekick offers AI-enhanced interpersonal coaching mediated by an app (Bailie & Butler, 2018).

IBM has taken these ideas one step further. An AI analyses employees' digital activities to infer their skills and proficiencies. This is cross-referenced against the future skills needs of the business identified through the strategic workforce planning process, and the information is used to provide employees with personal learning recommendations to employees. IBM claims that this has increased engagement with learning and has made it easier to fill vacancies internally. Machine learning is also used to inform managers' salary decisions (Moore & Bokelberg, 2019).

Defining the Role, Contribution, and Value of Talent in Organisations

The two examples—talent selection and talent development—discussed above reflect theories on how AI might be used in talent management (Strohmeier & Piazza, 2015) and examples emerging from practice. However, arguably, both are lacking in ambition—given the theoretical potential of AI for talent management. A key issue here is that, outside of the sphere of talent acquisition and selection, traditional talent management processes do not happen in sufficient quantity to generate the volume of data needed for working AI (Cappelli, Tambe, & Yakubovich, 2019). Therefore, a conceptual leap may be required if AI is to have a greater role in talent management. What might such a leap look like?

Doug Lemov is an educator and the author of a best-selling book on teaching (Lemov, 2015). His great insight was that no one knew what makes a good school teacher, so he set out to find out. He started by looking at data on school and pupil performance for evidence that might suggest if outstanding teachers were present in a school. He then observed how these outstanding teachers teach. As he watched more teachers, he identified common classroom practices that he thought explained their superior performance. Lemov's research journey closely mirrors that of an AI: look at the data, identify the top performers, look at what they do to pick out the things that they do that others do not, and predict the top performance. What, for Lemov, was a slow and time-consuming process could be accomplished by an AI in a fraction of that time, if it were fed data on pupil performance and videos of teachers' classroom practice. It is, therefore, possible to envisage workplaces of the future where worker performance and behaviour are observed by AI, which is in turn able to identify the behaviours needed for performance while recommending reward and promotion to those workers who display those behaviours.

If this sounds futuristic, in many workplaces, it is a piece of the future that has already arrived. Amazon recently attracted ignominy when it was revealed that it had automated decisions on firing low productivity workers in its fulfillment centres (Bort, 2019). However, the technology of the algorithmic direction of workers and constant real-time computer monitoring of worker performance (e.g., how many boxes have been moved through the warehouse and how quickly?) is already a well-established feature of the distribution industry (Bottani, Montanari, Rinaldi, & Vignali, 2015), and most large warehouse operators will make decisions on whether or not to terminate poor performers using such data, albeit in a less mechanistic fashion than Amazon.

In August 2019, DatasparQ—a London-based AI start-up—launched a new product aimed at British bars and pubs. It is a facial recognition system that tells the bar staff which customer to serve next, so that staff does not need to remember whose turn it is to be served. While this technology has the specific purpose of ensuring customers are served in the right order, once the infrastructure is in place, it could also easily be used for monitoring staff productivity and determining the behaviours that result in superior performance—as routinely happens in warehouses and as Doug Lemov did using observation and human judgement for teachers. The question then is will such technology catch on for the highly skilled knowledge workers that organisations have traditionally categorised as 'talent'?

A glimpse of one possible piece of the future is provided by Humanyze, a technology start-up specialising in 'sociometrics.' Humanyze's core product is to analyse human behaviour and interaction in the workplace: monitoring written electronic communication for employee sentiment, recording the length, tone, and emotion of speech, and monitoring physical movement and employee interaction using sociometric badges carried by each worker. The resulting data is then analysed to identify how to improve team performance. While Humanyze's focus is on team performance, it is not hard to see how such data could be used in talent management and development. In many ways, Humanyze represents a step-change in the use of technology to monitor the behaviour of knowledge workers. At the same time, it can be seen as a continuation and the development of technologies that have long been used to monitor the performance and behaviour of workers carrying out less-skilled jobs. The question then is will such technology come to occupy a central role in talent management in the future? To answer this question, it is necessary to consider the barriers and blockers to the adoption of AI in talent management. In the next section, we consider the role of data quality and availability, ethics, and legal risk and social norms, trust, and reputation and how these factors might limit the adoption of AI in talent management.

Barriers and Blockers

Data Quality and Availability

AIs require large volumes of high-quality data for training purposes (Von Krogh, 2018). Existing talent-related data held by organisations and needed to train AIs are, by the standards of 'Big Data,' small in size and of questionable quality. Data that could be considered pertinent to talent management includes electronic records of applications, selection decisions, performance reviews, and promotion and termination decisions. Even very large organisations do not make these decisions in the volume necessary to generate data large enough to train AI. However, issues of data size can be addressed by linking traditional talent data with other sources of data within the organisation, for example, from finance and operations (Cappelli et al., 2019) and new forms of data from cameras and sensors, like those described in the section above.

Existing talent data is also of questionable quality for two key reasons. First, the data are recorded electronically as a result of HR operations carried out through HRIS. Different users of HRIS will use these systems differently—completing some fields but not others; some entering zeros, others leaving fields blank, etc. Lack of consistency in data entry means that the data can only be analysed after time-consuming efforts to clean up the data and/or to ensure consistency in data entry. Soon, issues of data quality may be partially addressed by the adoption of AI within HRIS. The point of using AI in this way is to improve the speed and efficiency of HR operations (Guenole & Feinzig, 2019). One helpful consequence of such developments could be that the human role in data generation is mediated by AI, so that the AI generates digital traces and records of the activity in a more consistent and, therefore, higher-quality way rather than existing human operators. Second, data recorded represent efforts by managers to summarise a series of complex and frequently difficult to observe worker behaviours in simple multi-item scales (Cappelli et al., 2019). Such efforts will, therefore, be shot through with random measurement error and systematic biases (Buckingham, 2015). There is considerable concern that AI might encode and reproduce these systematic biases in a way that is impossible for humans to understand and is, therefore, a challenge (see the section 'Social norms, Trust, and

Reputation' below). However, the good news here is that AI also has the potential to learn to use random measurement error as instrumental variables that can identify and control more systematic biases (Cowgill, 2018), but only if there is data of sufficient volume and quality. Organisations also have to possess the will and inclination to want to use AI to overcome existing systemic biases (see the section 'Ethics and Risks of Discrimination' below). Overall then, as things currently stand in most organisations, talent data are not available in sufficient quantity or quality for AI to be applied in talent management. However, there is good reason to believe that this could change shortly.

Difficulties of Causal Inference

The availability of data is not in itself enough to facilitate the development of AI for talent management. Several other challenging issues also need to be resolved. At the heart of these is the point that AI specialises in making accurate predictions. However, prediction is distinct from causal inference, so precise prediction does not in itself provide a guide for appropriate action in the light of the prediction (Athey, 2018). For example, eBay massively overestimated the economic returns from online advertising through the use of a simple predictive model that did not account for the fact that many customers who purchased after clicking through to eBay's website from an advertisement would have purchased from eBay even if they had not clicked on the advertisement (Blake, Noski, & Tadelis, 2017). The cost of this mistake to eBay can be measured in unnecessary advertising expenses. The costs of making the same mistake in the field of talent management are likely to be much greater. If employees feel that they are being mistreated as a result of AI-driven talent decisions, then this will have demotivational effects on existing employees, damage the organisation's ability to attract and retain talent, and carry significant legal risks.

There are two basic approaches to making causal inferences. One is to ground predictive analysis in a theoretical model based on a deep knowledge of the issue in question. The second is to use randomised experiments to establish clear evidence of causality (Athey, 2018). Grounding predictive analysis from AIs within domain knowledge closely reflects the precepts of evidence-based management, which stresses the importance of using stakeholder concerns and values and professional expertise (Barends & Rousseau, 2018). The key question is how does this domain knowledge of talent management become embedded within the development and deployment of talent management AI? The structure of the emerging AI industry is one potential barrier. Most AI for HR and talent management are being developed by technology start-ups (Bailie & Butler, 2018). It, therefore, follows that AI for talent management will be adopted through procurement rather than through internal development. AI developers will therefore have to work very closely with clients to develop products that encode the necessary domain knowledge. It is an open question as to whether the structure of the industry can facilitate this level of close cooperation; the time that such cooperation takes may make it financially unattractive for customers. The potential need for bespoke AI talent management products for individual clients may make it harder for start-ups to raise development capital given that investors favour products that have the potential to scale rapidly.

Google has blazed a path for others to follow in using randomised experiments to make decisions about talent (Bock, 2015). One account suggests that workers will be willing to accept a role for random experiments in talent management AIs, because there is a widespread belief that talent decisions often involve luck rather than judgment (Cappelli et al., 2019). However, evidence suggests a more pessimistic view; people tend to disapprove of randomised experiments (Meyer et al., 2019). If this is the case, talent management AIs are likely to struggle to achieve acceptable levels of fairness and legitimacy.

Social Norms, Trust, and Reputation

This points to the broader challenge for talent management AIs. Will workers be prepared to trust AIs to influence their careers? Providing data for AIs to work with could involve workers giving up significant amounts of their privacy. Are they prepared to consent to employers creating and analysing digital records of every move they do at work and perhaps even outside of work too through the use of wearable technologies that record health, location, and activity data? Are they prepared to work for organisations where interpersonal decision-making about talent is replaced or augmented by AI-driven decisions? Will organisations be prepared to take the reputational and legal risks involved in adopting AI in talent management? Amazon has already attracted considerable opprobrium over the attempt of using AI in decisions about which employees to hire and fire (Bort, 2019; Dastin, 2018). Will this deter others from following the same path? There is a widespread perception that AIs trained on existing datasets are likely to encode existing social inequalities and biases—for example, against women, ethnic minorities, and the poor. For example, in response to an article on the use of AI for assessing candidates in job interviews, the technology journalist James O'Malley tweeted, 'there is no way this will not turn out to be racist'—a tweet that received 115,000 'likes' from other Twitter users. There is evidence that suggests that these concerns are not groundless; Internet search engines can systematically reproduce the racism of wider society (Noble, 2018). Although Cowgill (2018) demonstrates that it is technically possible for AI to learn not to discriminate in this way, there remain concerns that the technology industry will not enact the solutions, because those who work in it are blind to the problem (Wachter-Boettcher, 2017).

Ethics and Risks of Discrimination

Wider societal concerns about the ethics of data use and decision-making are encoded in national legal systems; therefore, employers are risking more than their reputation if they get AI wrong. In the European Union, the GDPR imposes several legal restrictions on the use and storage of employees' personal data—which could act as barriers to the development of talent management AI. First, the GDPR states that personal data should be collected for an explicit purpose with the permission of the person who the data is from and that it should not be used for other purposes without the explicit consent of the person whose data it is (Butterworth, 2018:260). This means that organisations can only start to collect potential training data for talent AIs with the explicit permission of employees; they cannot merely feed data from existing HR and enterprise information systems into the AI. Second, organisations are expected to understand the impact of using AI or any other data processing activity on the different groups affected. It is therefore incumbent on organisations to be able to explain how, for example, ethnic minorities are treated by the AI in comparison to white employees and to be able to demonstrate that there is a legitimate reason for any differences in treatment (Butterworth, 2018; Goodman & Flaxman, 2017). Similar considerations apply in the United States, where organisations need to be careful not to fall foul of civil rights legislation that outlaws discrimination against women and ethnic minorities (Scherer, 2017). While smaller organisations that do not operate in the European Union or the United States may be able to avoid such legal regulation, large organisations with operations that are global in scope—precisely the sort of organisation with the resources and scale economies to make AI an attractive investment—are likely needed to comply.

Conclusions

The use of technology for people management decision-making is advancing rapidly with the development of artificial intelligence. This chapter has reviewed how AI might be used, is being used, and could be used in talent management. Initial applications of AI focus on supporting decision-making over candidate selection, but it is possible to envisage much more far-reaching uses for the technology. However, if these applications are to be developed in practice, there are scientific, social, ethical, and legal barriers to be overcome. Can talent AI be sufficiently grounded in an understanding of causality? Will employees consent to their data being used in talent AIs, and will they agree to the role of AI in decision-making over their careers? Will the results of talent AIs comply with legal regulations that aim to ensure fairness in data processing?

These questions raise challenges for both academics and talent management practitioners. Perhaps, the key problem for talent management professionals is to ensure that their professional expertise and ethics are encoded into new AI talent management tools as they develop. The current risk is that these tools are developed by computer scientists to serve the interest of operational and financial managers who do not understand talent and rather see people as a cost to be minimised as compared to the key to competitive advantage while reproducing discriminatory practices against women and minority groups. For academics, there are challenges in researching and generating knowledge about new AI-enabled approaches to talent management. How can we see through the fog of hype around AI in talent management being generated by start-ups, technology companies, and their sponsors while also peering past the screens of commercial confidentiality that organisations are deploying these tools erect? In making sense of data, can we avoid the twin perils of excessive pessimism engendered by theory and evidence that shows how algorithms can be tools for oppression and inequality and baseless optimism arising from industry hype? The use of AI in talent management could become the key differentiator of successful organisations in the near future, but there are formidable challenges to be overcome to make this vision a reality. Ultimately, the use of AI in talent management is likely to reflect the values of the businesses introducing it and the societies they operate in. Therefore we all have a responsibility to speak up for the values that matter to us.

References

Agrawal, A., Gans, J., & Goldfarb, A. (2018). *Prediction machines: The simple economics of artificial intelligence.* Boston, MA: Harvard Business Review Press.

Agrawal, A., Gans, J., & Goldfarb, A. (2019). *Artificial intelligence: The ambiguous labour market impact of automatic prediction.* Working Paper 25619. Boston, MA: National Bureau of Economic Research.

Athey, S. (2018). Beyond prediction: Using big data for policy problems. *Science, 335*(6324), 483–485.

Bailie, I., & Butler, M. M. (2018). *An examination of artificial intelligence and its impact on human resources.* London: Cognition X.

Barends, E., & Rousseau, D. (2018). *Evidence-based management: How to use evidence to make better organisational decision.* London: Kogan Page.

Blake, T., Noski, S., & Tadelis, S. (2017). Consumer heterogeneity and paid search effectiveness: A large scale field experiment. *Econometrica, 83*(1), 155–174.

Bock, L. (2015). *Work rules.* London: John Murray.

Bort, J. (2019). Amazon's warehouse-worker tracking system can automatically pick people to fire without a human supervisor's involvement. *Business Insider.* 25 Apr 2019. Retrieved from: https://www.businessinsider.com/amazon-system-automatically-fires-warehouse-workers-time-off-task-2019-4?r=US&IR=T.

Bottani, E., Montanari, R., Rinaldi, M., & Vignali, G. (2015). Intelligent algorithms for warehouse management. Intelligent techniques in engineering management. In C. Kahramen & S. C. Onar (Eds.), *Intelligent techniques in engineering management* (pp. 645–647). New York, NY: Springer.

Brynjolfsson, E., Rock, D., & Syverson, C. (2017). *Artificial intelligence and the modern productivity paradox: A clash of expectations and statistics.* Working Paper 24001. Boston, MA: National Bureau of Economic Research.

Buckingham, M. (2015). *Most HR data is bad data.* Harvard Business Review, February.

Butterworth, M. (2018). The ICO and artificial intelligence: The role of fairness in the GDPR framework. *Computer Law and Security Review, 34*(2), 257–268.

Cappelli, P., Tambe, P., & Yakubovich, V. (2019). Artificial intelligence in human resources management: Challenges and a path forward. Retrieved from https://dx.doi.org/10.2139/ssrn.3263878.

Cookson, C. (2018). DeepMind in AI breakthrough with smarter version of AlphaGo. *Financial Times,* 6 Dec 2018. Retrieved from https://www.ft.com/content/ac50f12a-f962-11e8-af46-2022a0b02a6c.

Cowgill, B. (2018). *Bias and productivity in humans and algorithms: Theory and evidence from resume screening.* Columbia University Working Paper. Retrieved from http://conference.iza.org/conference_files/MacroEcon_2017/cowgill_b8981.pdf.

Dastin, J. (2018). Amazon scraps secret AI recruiting tool that showed bias against women. *Reuters*, 10 Oct 2018. Retrieved from https://www.reuters.com/article/us-amazon-com-jobs-automation-insight/amazon-scraps-secret-ai-recruiting-tool-that-showed-bias-against-women-idUSKCN1MK08G.

Goodman, B., & Flaxman, S. (2017). European union regulations on algorithmic decision-making and a 'right to explanation'. *AI Magazine*, *38*(3), 50–57.

Guenole, N., & Feinzig, S. (2019). *The business case for AI in HR*. IBM Smarter Workforce Institute.

Highhouse, S. (2008). Stubborn reliance on intuition and subjectivity in employee selection. *Industrial and Organizational Psychology*, *1*, 333–342. 10.1111/j.1754-9434.2008.00058.x.

Lemov, D. (2015). *Teach like a champion 2.0*. San Francisco, CA: Jossey Bass.

Meyer, N. M., Heck, P. R., Holtzman, G. M., Anderson, S. M., Cai, W., Watts, D. J., & Chabris, C. J. (2019). Objecting to experiments that compare two unobjectionable policies or treatments. *Proceedings of the National Academy of Sciences*, *116*(22), 10723–10728.

Moore, T., & Bokelberg, E. (2019). How IBM incorporates artificial intelligence into strategic workforce planning. *People and Strategy Journal*, Fall. Retrieved from https://www.hrps.org/resources/people-strategy-journal/Fall2019/Pages/moore-bokelberg-feature.aspx.

Noble, S. U. (2018). *Algorithms of oppression*, New York, NY: NYU Press.

O'Malley, J. (2019). Tweet on 1st October. Retrieved from https://twitter.com/Psythor/status/1178926854868213760?s=20.

Scherer, M. (2017). AI in HR: Civil rights implications of employers' use of artificial intelligence and big data. *SciTech Lawyer*, *13*(2), 12–15.

Simms, J. (2019). AI versus HR. *Work*, *2019*, 14–18.

Somers, J. (2017). Is AI a one trick pony? *MIT Technology Review*, 29 Sep 2017. Retrieved from https://www.technologyreview.com/2017/09/29/67852/is-ai-riding-a-one-trick-pony/.

Strohmeier, S. & Piazza, F. (2015). Artificial intelligence techniques in human resource management: A conceptual exploration. *Intelligent Techniques in Engineering Management*, *87*, 149–172.

Von Krogh, G. (2018). Artificial intelligence in organisations: New opportunities for phenomenon-based theorizing. *Academy of Management Discoveries*, *4*(4), 404–409.

Wachter-Boettcher, S. (2017). *Technically wrong: Sexist apps, biased algorithms, and other threats of toxic tech*. New York, NY: W.W. Norton.

Index

Printed in the United States
by Baker & Taylor Publisher Services